Parents In Love

Reclaiming Intimacy After Your Child Is Born

Linda Salazar

*To Stephanie
Best Wishes
Linda Salazar*

Kystar Publishing

Parents in Love: Reclaiming Intimacy After Your Child Is Born
Copyright © 1998 by Linda Salazar

All rights reserved. No part of this book may be reproduced or transmitted in any form or by any means, electronic or mechanical, including photocopying, recording, or by any information storage and retrieval system without written permission from the author, except for the inclusion of quotations in a review.

For information contact: Kystar Publishing
P. O. Box 3501
Rolling Hills Estates, CA 90274

Grateful acknowledgement is made for permission to reprint the poem, *To Betsy,* written by Ric Giardina © 1996.

Cover by Robert Howard

Printed in U.S.A.

Library of Congress Catalogue Card Number: 98-91210
ISBN: 0-9662250-0-7

First Edition

10 9 8 7 6 5 4 3 2 1

Dedication

To Jim, my husband, lover, partner, best friend. Thank you for your everlasting support and love and for your constant belief in us as a couple and as parents. You have been my greatest teacher.

I love you.

Acknowledgments

This book was made possible by the love and support from the following people in my life:

Jack Barnard, my funny, talented, and brilliant editor, who kept my spirits high and helped me find my writing voice. Thank you for making this fun.

Darla Isackson, whose editing contributions and manuscript suggestions helped create the final project. Thank you for your heartfelt kindness and expertise.

Peggy Peterka of Business Ink, whose endless hours of dedication shaped the manuscript into book form. Thank you for your unwavering patience and professionalism.

Hal Zina Bennett and Susan Sparrow, two wonderful writers, whose willingness to share their knowledge, exemplifies the special people that they are. Thank you for your input and answering all my questions.

Ulyssa Childs, Laurel Stutsman, Adrienne Lopez, and Marcia Craig-Smith, whose friendship and belief in me, mean everything to me. Thank you for taking the time out of your busy lives to read the manuscript and share your honest opinions.

All the parents I interviewed, whose stories helped make this book possible. Thank you for your honesty, openness and willingness to trust me.

My parents, Chuck and Joyce Kaplan, whose support throughout my life is appreciated more than words can say. Thank you for your love.

My son, Kyle, who has brought me more joy and happiness in my life than I could have ever imagined. Thank you for putting up with my endless hours on the computer, for your shining smile, your humor, and for teaching me what unconditional love is really about. I love you.

My husband, Jim, whose patience throughout this whole project has been astounding. Thank you for sharing your life with me.

Contents

	Introduction..9	
1.	Be Patient with Me and Forgive My Mistakes	15
2.	Who Am I Now?..	26
3.	Parent Trap	33
4.	Magical Moments	41
5.	Who's Got the Time!...	51
6.	I Need, You Need; Now What?	63
7.	Sex—What Sex?	73
8.	Talk To Me; I'm Listening	85
9.	Dreams Are Forever	97
10.	Words of Wisdom	105
	Closing................................... 119	
	Afterword.............................. 125	

Introduction

From pure, unadulterated pain to total ecstasy—in a split second. What a feeling! The minute I laid eyes on my newborn son, my life was as complete as I'd ever dreamed it could be. My husband was by my side with tears in his eyes, wearing a smile as big as a kid would have on his birthday. The depth of love I felt for him and our son was something I'd never before experienced. My dreams, hopes, and expectations had all come together in one miraculous moment.

Experiencing the birth of a child is absolutely one of life's greatest gifts; one of the few times in adult life when you are most likely to let down your guard and allow yourself to be truly intimate with your partner. You become as naked as the newborn child who just entered your life.

As I held Kyle, with Jim next to me, I knew that nothing in my life could ever match that feeling, and I wondered if my husband and I would ever feel this connected again.

That was then and this is now. Ten years later, with those memories etched in our hearts, we continue the journey of raising our son. The closeness Jim and I felt on March 12, 1988, hasn't since been equaled; and yet, I've realized our relationship has grown and matured in ways I never dreamed possible.

The transformations that have taken place in me and in our relationship have brought us many surprises, and, of course, many challenges with every step we have taken. As we watch Kyle grow, we learn something new every day and discover how to live our lives in the present, not from the past.

I've written this book with the hope of easing the struggle that so many parents experience in their relationships after parenthood. In order to accomplish this I used not only my own experiences but those of other parents. Throughout, I've included enlightening insights from some of the 100 men and women I've interviewed about the amazing changes parenthood has brought into their lives.

As you might imagine, the parenting experiences of these couples were quite diverse. Some grew in all areas of life and became closer. Others questioned their decisions, believing that having children increased the emotional distance in their relationships. Given the opportunity to become parents all over again, a handful said they would not. For them, the stress on their relationship has been too painful; yet, in the same breath they expressed how much they loved their children, in spite of it all.

Almost all of the parents were concerned about the lack of time left in their lives after the demands of childcare. The all-encompassing nature of parenthood caught them completely off guard; they felt totally unprepared.

PREPARATION

Think about the feeling of being unprepared for a moment. During the nine months of pregnancy most expectant mothers continue to live their lives as they normally would, doing the things they like to do—going out, traveling, reading, doing whatever makes them happy. As a matter of fact, mothers-to-be often pamper themselves, taking extra care of themselves to ensure the health of their children.

During those nine months before a child's birth, your relationship may even become stronger while the two of you experience the stages of pregnancy as your child grows inside of Mom. You allow yourselves to fantasize about all the tender moments you'll share as a family.

Then suddenly, you're parents! In a flash, you realize there was nothing you could have done to sufficiently prepare yourselves for all the incredible demands now infringing on your time.

Traditionally, preparing for your baby means: painting the nursery, picking out furniture, choosing a name, having a baby shower, going through birthing classes, and reading parenting books. But none of those projects helps you prepare for the changes in your life with your partner. So the question still remains, what *can* you do to prepare for those changes? The obvious answer is, buy this book or have a kind, loving friend buy it for you. (All right, maybe that's a little *too* obvious.)

The real answer is: you *can't* adequately prepare ahead of time for these changes, either personally or between the two of you. Sleeping late every weekend till the baby comes won't keep you from needing sleep during the next six months. You can't store up enough time with your partner on pre-children dates so you won't need to go out again for a few years. Spending time by yourself enjoying all your favorite pastimes doesn't satisfy the need to be by yourself after the baby comes. Telling your partner how much you appreciate him or her doesn't eliminate the need for acknowledgment once you're parents. You certainly can't cram in enough dream vacations before kids so you won't need another one until they're out of the house.

And if you believe you can have mock arguments "before baby" that in any way resemble arguments "after baby," forget it. I can hear it now. "Uh oh, sweetpea, here's that situation we created during one of our make-believe arguments. Remember what we decided, dear?"

"Oh yeah, no problem, darling, I'll get right on it. I'm sorry I forgot."

Give it up. It will *never* happen.

You can't prepare yourselves for the millions of needs your baby will have, or even the new needs the two of you will have. You see, you have no idea how either of you are going to feel when this child enters your lives. You have no idea what your child's personality will be, or what this precious treasure needs. You have no idea how you or your partner will respond to this new role. You don't even know how you'll respond to each other.

With all there is to learn and all the changes that take place, trials and tribulations are inevitable. Just as inevitable are the shifts in the relationships after couples have children.

Whether conscious of it or not, you're not the same two people you were before you had children. Your values and beliefs change a little or a lot. You no longer look at your own parents in the same way. Suddenly, you may understand why they did what they did, even though you may choose not to do the same things all over again. You may see parts of your partner that you never knew existed. Some of these parts you like and some you don't. New fears show up. Your needs change and maybe you're not sure how to express them—some things that seemed so important before are no longer important to you now. Your sex life shifts gears and you wonder if you'll ever get it back into drive. *Everything* changes.

The challenge in life now is not just about being a good parent. The challenge is also about learning to be with and interact with your partner from a whole new place—a place where you deepen your intimacy. As you move from the comfortable world of just the two of you to the unfamiliar world of parenthood, ask yourself: am I willing to express to my partner what I'm experiencing in this stage of our lives so we *can* move to that deeper level?

This means expressing the joy as well as the confusion, fears, anger, and disappointments—all of which can be felt throughout your parenting journey. Not sharing some of these feelings keeps you from strengthening your love and often makes it weaker.

Give yourselves time to learn about each other in your new roles. The love you share for your children presents you with the opportunity to give birth to an extraordinary relationship with your lover. In addition, you now have the chance to become the example that teaches your kids how to have such a relationship in their adult lives.

As you read this book, open your heart. Explore my words so that they reach the deepest parts of your being. I hope to bring new ideas into your personal awareness and into your relationship, sparking your desire to grow in areas you thought couldn't evolve any further. I hope to make you laugh at times, because laughter is a crucial ingredient for building a loving family. (Let's face it, laughter is a critical ingredient for *all* aspects of life.)

Keep in mind that with all the changes you go through, growth emerges for the individuals as well as for the couple. Now that you're a parent, let this book help you discover your highest intention in your relationship with your partner.

~1~

Be Patient with Me and Forgive My Mistakes

"A child learns and explores with no sense of failure or limit. Recovering that child within us is the key to accelerated learning."

David Meier

Finally, we're home from the hospital! I enter the house with Kyle cradled safely in my arms, and, aware of my precious cargo, I carefully climb the stairs. I have so looked forward to this naptime—my newborn baby snuggled against my body—the two of us alone together. The moment I've dreamed of has finally arrived.

Before settling down to sleep, I decide to change Kyle's diaper. Gently laying him on the bed, I unwrap the blanket from around his delicate body. He shivers. Quickly, I remove his wet diaper and replace it with a dry one. I whisper in his ear, "Time to bundle you up again, my little gem, so you'll be cozy and warm."

As I kiss his tender cheek, I prepare to wrap him back up in his blanket. "Now, exactly how did Daddy and those nice nurses swaddle you in this blanky?" Attempting to repeat what they did, I find myself unsuccessful the first time. I straighten out the blanket and try again. No luck. Kyle is still shivering and I'm sweating. "Mommy loves you," I tell him. "I'll figure this out. Hang in there with me." With yet another failed attempt, he becomes irritated and starts to cry. I panic. I need to get my baby warm. "O.K., Linda," I say to myself. "Calm down. You can do this."

After five minutes I crumble, falling face down next to Kyle, and we cry in unison. Jim comes flying up the stairs. "What's going on? What's the matter?" Through my tears I say, "I can't do this. I'm no good. You be the mother. I'm going back to work. I can't even get my baby warm. How am I supposed to take care of him if I can't do something as simple as wrapping him up in his blanket?"

Jim realizes I'm just a wee bit on edge and takes the blanket. Effortlessly he swaddles Kyle, who stops crying immediately, and places him in the bassinet next to our bed. I look at Jim with the eyes of a lost puppy. He kisses my forehead and tells me to get some rest. "Don't worry," he says with a gleam in his eyes, "you're going to be a great mom and I'm sure you'll be the best swaddler in the neighborhood. Before you know it, we'll be entering you in the National Swaddler Contest."

He leaves the room and I lie back on the bed. With tears still falling down my cheeks, I look over at my new pride and joy. "Sweetheart," I say softly, "I've got a lot to learn, but I promise I'll learn it. Be patient with me and forgive my mistakes. Sleep tight, my little prince."

"Be patient with me and forgive my mistakes." These words should go home with all new parents as they leave the hospital. Then, once home, they should be immediately taped on the bedroom ceilings so they are the last thing moms and dads see at night and the first thing they see in the morning.

When it comes to new experiences, no matter how many books you read or how many classes you take, there is nothing that gives you the skills to accomplish the task like the actual doing. The more you do something, the more comfortable you become and the better you are at it. Think back on all the times you started something new in your life: a job, school, a sport, driving—they all had their ups and downs. With each of those new ventures there was someone to teach or coach you along the way. You needed someone to encourage you.

Your first experience with parenting is no different. There are going to be times when you're struggling and other moments when you feel you've been a parent forever. What you need to remember is that you and your partner are each others' primary support system. Yes, it's important to include grandparents and close friends. Their experience and help can be beneficial. However, this is still *your* child. *You* are the parents. *You two* will have to learn what's best for your son or daughter.

You should be each other's biggest cheerleaders. I know how hard that can be at times—especially with all the emotional changes you're going through. But the fact still remains, you're experiencing this learning curve together and patience and forgiveness should be your highest priorities. Give yourselves a break!

This goes double for women who may have left a fulfilling career, women who were used to handling twenty things at once. You can forget about trying to maintain that level of expertise for a while. I know you didn't step into your office job and become instantly capable of managing twenty things at once. You worked your way toward that level of expertise gradually. The same holds true with learning the skills of parenthood—it's a gradual process and you learn as you go.

Many stay-at-home moms tell me they aren't good with their new responsibilities, such as taking care of their babies, the housework, laundry, and cooking. They feel they aren't accomplishing anything—perhaps because most household and mothering tasks don't *stay* done. For example, you just change a diaper or do the dishes, and it's time to do it again. And to make matters worse, you can't find the time to get out of your pajamas or take a shower. One mom said she was ecstatic when she paid three bills in one day and couldn't wait to tell her husband when he came home. It's normal for you new mothers to feel like you've wasted your whole day on mundane, recurring tasks, if you're used to accomplishing big goals.

Suggestion: Stop fighting motherhood. Embrace it. Your whole outlook will change. You *will* do what *needs* to get done. Some days, that may simply be keeping your baby happy and feeling loved. (The horror!) You'll find yourself just being Mom and not some super hero.

LEARNING YOUR WAY

There was a woman in one of my seminars who took on the job of motherhood with great ease. She handled everything at home and was extremely organized about it. The only problem she had was her husband, who was having a hard time learning how to be the daddy. He attempted to help with the baby and in the process did some things differently than his wife did them. When this happened, she would stop him, take over, and show him the "right" way.

Needless to say, that left Dad frustrated and he quit pitching in. Mom couldn't understand this. She believed she was *helping* him by saving him the aggravation of trying to figure out a baby issue for himself. After all, she was with the baby all day, every day, and knew her son's every need.

That approach doesn't make for a happy relationship. It not only keeps you on opposite teams, but your partner may lose all desire to contribute.

Dad, if this is happening to you and you're not happy, speak up. Let Mom know that you appreciate her input, but you'd like to do it your own way for now—that if you need her help, you'll ask for it. And Mom, if you happen to be in the same room when Dad's dealing with the baby, I have three words for you: leave the room! Make that four words: *leave the room now!* He'll be more relaxed and you'll be less tempted to interfere. Dad, you do the same. When Mom's having a hard time with the baby and doesn't want help, go do something else around the house—or you may be taking your life in your hands. (You know how those postpartum mothers can be. One second they're calm and the next second they're flinging used baby wipes at you.)

If I could have swaddled Kyle in his blanket that first time, I would have been thrilled. But I couldn't, so I asked Jim to teach me (after I stopped crying and had some sleep, of course). He loved teaching me and I was ready to learn. And here's the lesson to remember: when we're not ready to listen we won't learn anything, anyway.

If Mom's home all day and Dad works full time, he should be given as much of an opportunity as possible to be alone with the baby when he is home. He'll not only learn to care for Junior the way he wants to, but they'll also build a wonderful bond. Psst, Mom! Try not to leave all sorts of instructions. Trust that the father of your child can do this. He's a grown man. If you come home and the baby's screaming and Dad seems fine, don't rush over and grab the baby. Talk to Dad first; remember, you don't know what's been happening. If he wants you to take the baby, make sure you keep him involved. Don't just push him away, unless, of course, he's begging to be relieved. Support, support, support. Do whatever you can together. A parenting team that strives to be the best they can wins the brass pacifier.

"We cannot direct the wind, but we can adjust our sails." This Chinese proverb on flexibility can come in very handy during the learning stage. By the way, I'm still learning about parenthood ten years later. There are no set rules for raising a child. You and your partner will create your own, and if they work for both of you, great! If you've been doing something that doesn't seem to work and your partner has a better way—change *your* way. Don't plant your feet in old baby poop. And just because something worked in the past doesn't mean it will work again. This is about give and take and "two heads are better than one." Praise your partner when he or she solves a baby problem that you couldn't figure out.

Sometimes you'll feel that praise isn't deserved, that your partner isn't getting the hang of this parenting thing as quickly as you'd like. Or perhaps you're not getting the help you expected. Before you know it, you're complaining to other parents and they're boasting about how wonderful *their* partners are. The tendency here is to compare your mate to someone else's. Don't. You'll get nowhere fast, and if your partner finds out, they'll be deeply hurt. The truth is, you don't have a clue what goes on in someone else's life on a daily basis. What you're hearing is edited information.

THE BIG SECRET

I hope you're sitting down because I'm about to share something with you that may shatter your entire fantasy world. Are you ready? Here we go. *There is no perfect parent. There is no perfect relationship.* There, I said it. I'll wait to continue until I have your attention again. Go ahead. Get a glass of water. Calm yourself down.

O.K., let's go on.

During any learning process we can become overwhelmed. Some of us handle the overwhelm better than others, which helps us learn quicker. As I mentioned earlier, I'm still learning about parenthood ten years later and I still have the teen years ahead! As Kyle gets older, Jim and I have to search for new ways to do things when the old ways stop being effective.

There are moments when we feel overpowered by the necessities of our lives. Jim and I do whatever we can to help each other through these periods. That means accepting mistakes, offering suggestions without making them mandatory, being flexible, and having a great deal of patience and understanding with one another. We both have our strengths and weaknesses, just as you and your partner do.

If you learn from those strengths and support each other during times of weakness, you'll become a team no one can split up. The key is: "be patient and forgive the mistakes."

> *"I'm only human, and therefore I will make mistakes. Each mistake is an opportunity to learn and increase my level of awareness."*
> Ellen Kreidman
> *How Can We Light a Fire When The Kids Are Driving Us Crazy?*

EXERCISE:
1. Write down what you believe to be your biggest struggle as a parent.

2. Share what you've written with your partner and discuss how you can eliminate or lessen your struggle.

3. Write down what you believe to be your partner's greatest strengths as a parent.

4. Share with your partner what you've written. This lets your partner know you're aware of those strengths and he or she will feel appreciated.

~2~

Who Am I Now?

"There is a process after children are in our lives. We go through a separation, transformation, and emergence within ourselves."
Susan Monk
When The Heart Waits

Imagine this scene: Two years after Kyle's birth I'm sitting with my favorite husband in my favorite restaurant eating my favorite breakfast. Suddenly, from nowhere, for no apparent reason, the tears start—plopping drop-by-drop into my cinnamon swirl French toast.

Why? What prompted such an emotion? We were merely discussing the possibility of moving to the Northwest to raise Kyle. "Maybe we could open up a hardware store," Jim said to me. "I could run it; you could keep the books. You're good at that." This was the moment my teardrops began drowning my French toast. Sure, the thought of moving out of L.A. was appealing. Even the idea of leaving my present work in the film industry was exciting enough, but becoming a bookkeeper? Ahh . . . that was another issue.

So I cried into my toast, while my poor husband sat there with a kind of Elmer Fudd look on his face. The way I was carrying on you'd think Jim was telling me that having Kyle was the biggest mistake he ever made and he was leaving us. That wasn't the case at all. We were simply discussing moving and doing something different with our careers. Prior to this conversation, I was fine with the possibility and now we were just throwing more ideas around.

Nevertheless, I was feeling depressed and confused and didn't understand exactly why. Something was happening inside of me that had been building up ever since Kyle was born. Every cell in my body was different. I was transforming in a very unfamiliar way and it scared me.

About six months after my son came into my life I realized I was not the same person as I had been before Kyle. Or maybe this person was always a part of me and she was just now revealing herself. Either way, I knew I couldn't go back to who I was before becoming a parent. I needed to make some changes in my life; I just didn't know what those changes should be. Having Kyle sparked the idea that I wanted to contribute something more to society. I was feeling things I had never felt before. I had a new-found love and compassion for people. I was thinking about the future of the world in ways that went beyond my former thinking, and instead of seeing my thoughts just pass by like leaves in a stream, they begged for action.

As difficult as this journey was for me, it was doubly hard for Jim. It brought many exasperating moments into our relationship that may never have come up without Kyle in our lives. My bouts of depression and frustration created a great deal of tension between us. I wasn't able to explain myself. There was nothing Jim could do for me to make me feel better, and that was frustrating for him.

There were moments in the relationship when I felt isolated, lonely, and misunderstood. Periodically, I was overwhelmed because I needed time to myself and that's exactly what I no longer had. I was afraid to talk about my feelings because I wasn't sure what they were. The words I needed in order to express how I felt didn't seem to exist. All I could say was, "I'm unhappy," and then I'd start crying again. (Understand this was not about postpartum depression. That period had come and gone already. This was much bigger.)

How could I feel this way? I had a husband who adored me, a beautiful, healthy son, a good career, a home I loved, friends who supported me. Why should I be this unhappy? It felt crazy to be this miserable. Everything on the outside was so wonderful, but the inside was topsy turvy.

Then it hit me. It's the inside that counts, not the outside. I began to embrace this old cliché and whether it made sense or not, it gave me what I needed to start sharing my confusion with Jim. When I succeeded at sharing, I felt a shift take place inside. All I had needed was a sounding board. I didn't need anyone to fix anything because nothing was broken. (Actually, everything was new and in perfect condition. I just wasn't familiar with the parts yet.)

Not long after this awakening I found myself crawling out of my black hole. I could see glimpses of light. Jim's silent support was great medicine. He listened while I talked. I began sharing my feelings with other mothers only to find they were going through a similar process. It was a slow trek, but after about a year and a half I could feel the sun on my skin again.

As you feel yourself changing, it's of paramount

importance to talk to each other. Let your partner know what you're thinking about, where your confusion lies, how you see yourself now that you're a parent, what you miss, what you wish you could have back again.

Many parents shared with me that they felt as though they had lost their childhood, others that they had regained it. Some of the dads were intimidated by their children. Others suddenly felt old and saw their own fathers when they looked in the mirror. Many moms struggled with whether to go back to work. One part of them wanted to and another didn't.

Feelings like this are common. The prescription is simple: allow yourself to feel the emotion and know that you will eventually find your place in this new venture. Take it one day at a time, one hour at a time, if need be. Just keep the lines of communication clear, because if you don't, it's way too easy to misread each other. You'll find yourself jumping to conclusions, making your partner wrong, and creating arguments that have no truth to them.

You're in a life transition and there's no way around it. Let your partner know your relationship is fine, that you just need some space right now; and above all, consistently acknowledge your love for one another.

Just as your children go through growth spurts, you're going through one, too. It takes time and patience before you reach a maturity level where you feel whole again and can move forward in your life. And I guarantee you this, as your children move into different phases of their lives, *your growth spurts will continue.*

One thing I can't stress enough: the more you're willing to talk, the quicker you heal. To shed some new light, these conversations don't always have to be with your partner. Talk to other parents, your own parents, whoever you feel safe with. Writing also helps to move your emotions. Meditating or just sitting quietly can bring new revelation; it was during a quiet moment that I decided to write this book.

Let your new differences just *be*. Befriend them. Bring them deep into your heart and soul. Love them; allow them to heal you.

When I was going through my "life change," many, many times I blamed my husband for my unhappiness and wondered if our marriage would survive. Don't do this. This isn't about blame. It's about change, and when you change, so will your relationship.

Be there for each other. If you come from your heart with your experiences, you'll see your relationship prosper because of the changes. You can't stay the same two people you were before having kids—it's just not possible. You may find yourself more loving and patient after kids, or perhaps you need to grow into that way of being. Either way, you're still changing.

Remember the importance of cherishing the past while learning to embrace the present. A wonderful quote from Deepak Chopra lets us know how important the present is: "The past is history, the future is a mystery, and this moment is a gift. That is why this moment is called 'the present'."

I'm going to end this chapter with another quote that says what I want to say very succinctly.

> *"Stop worrying about who you think you should be and start listening for an altogether new kind of voice that has been quietly calling to you. Let it show you where to find yourself."*
>
> Guy Finley
> The Secret of Letting Go

EXERCISE:
1. Write down any emotional changes you're feeling since parenthood.

2. Read what you've written to your partner and explore the best ways for you to be helped through this transition.

~3~

Parent Trap

"Nothing has a stronger influence on the children than the unlived life of the parents"
Carl Jung

The sun is out; a light breeze blows overhead. As I lay on the grass, watching the gossamer clouds float by, I find myself gently, sweetly moving towards them. The closer I get, the lighter I feel. Peacefulness flows throughout my body. Ahh . . . Crash! What's going on? Where am I? One eye opens to reveal a smiling, bubbling three-year-old boy jumping up and down at the foot of my bed, rambling away about putting his new train set together. The other eye searches for the clock: 6:00 A.M.! This rambunctious boy didn't get to bed until midnight; Jim and I followed an hour later. How could our adorable energy ball possibly be awake at this insane hour?

Then it hits me like a snowball in the face: It's Christmas morning. Kyle got a new train on Christmas Eve, and he's intent on getting it up and running.

With the persistence that is unique to children, Kyle manages to drag Jim out of bed and down the stairs to put his precious train together. Knowing how tired Jim must be, I find myself thinking how sweet he is to be doing this for Kyle. Instead of just lying in bed, I'm going to record this tender moment on video. After all, dad and son putting a train set together is right out of a storybook. As I'm getting up to get my camcorder, less-than-pleasant noises from downstairs tell me that the moment is over. Something ugly has developed. Something that is not out of a storybook and should definitely not be recorded on video tape.

In the den I find a very exhausted, very frustrated father who wants nothing more than to be sawing logs in our warm, comfy bed. Before I can react, Jim starts yelling—about the time, about the train not working properly, about being controlled by a three-year-old. Instead of keeping calm, I yell back and Kyle begins to sob. So much for a Merry Christmas.

We finally manage to gain our composure and things settle down. Jim stays to himself and I do everything in my power to avoid him, keeping Kyle close by my side. We're scheduled to go to Jim's sister's home for a family Christmas brunch; in silence, we prepare to leave. Of course, the air is so thick you could cut it with a chain saw.

As I get into the car, I realize we're in no mood to be with Jim's family. Leaving Jim in the car, I march inside with Kyle, call Jim's sister and explain why we aren't coming. I put Kyle down for a nap and when Jim finally comes back into the house I find the courage to sit down with him to talk about what happened. I use the word *courage* because I've never seen my husband this upset and I'm afraid of what he might say during our conversation.

What I discover is how trapped he's feeling in his life. "All I ever do anymore is go to work, come home, deal with Kyle, go to bed, get up the next morning and start the whole routine all over again. There's no fun in life anymore. There's no time for me, for us. I love my little boy and I love you, but I feel trapped." Bingo! Trapped. Suddenly, everything sounds very familiar. I've felt the same way many times since becoming a mom. We continue to talk all the way through Kyle's nap to resolve the issue—a two-hour conversation. In the end, we did have a very Merry Christmas and I gave Jim all the space he needed that day.

As parents, we all have the feeling of being trapped at one time or another. We go through life caught up in our daily responsibilities with no breaks: work, kids, household chores, sleep, work, kids, chores, sleep—and we start believing that's what life's all about.

This is when the parent trap snaps shut. With no warning, we explode, hurting everyone around us and leaving them and us fragmented. The only way to put the pieces together again is to reveal what caused the explosion in the first place.

How the exploding parent expresses him or herself determines the partner's response—either negative or positive. When Jim explained his feelings, he didn't blame me or Kyle. He simply shared how he felt and took responsibility for his blowup that morning. This made it easy for me to listen and want to help in any way I could.

If you don't watch for the signs or listen to your inner voice that softly says, "I wish I had more time; I wish I had my life back," the parent trap may snap shut without you recognizing it. That voice is there for a reason. Acknowledge your feelings and let your partner know what you need so that you both can take action.

Imagine if you were bold enough to take a day off work and do whatever you wanted. One day can do wonders for the soul. What if you and your honey took the day off to spend together. It can happen. It's been done before. (Believe it or not, I know people who have actually done this and weren't fired.)

The point is, when you have a child, you don't have to stop living your life. You *can* continue and *should* continue to do many of the things you did before. It's true that in the first few months your child needs all of your attention. But when you've become more comfortable as a parent, engage in some of your favorite pastimes again.

I love horseback riding and I rode until I was seven months pregnant. When I was fearful of falling off the horse and hurting the baby, I stopped. After I had Kyle, I didn't ride again for six months. That was a big mistake. I felt as though I couldn't have any more fun in my life. I wasn't doing anything I did before Kyle. I kept asking myself, "Why can't I do the things *I* like to do? Does everything have to be about motherhood?"

Jim realized that I needed to do something for myself and suggested I get back on a horse. My excuses were a mile long: "What would I do with Kyle? What if I can't get a lesson during his nap time? Who would watch him, anyway? What if he starts crying? What if I fall off the horse, hurt myself, and can't take care of my son? We need to save money. I shouldn't spend it on lessons. What if the horse starts galloping and doesn't stop until it reaches Disneyland?" I just went on and on.

Luckily, my husband addressed all of my concerns and I found a wonderful teacher who was willing to hold Kyle during the whole lesson, if necessary. Without the excuses standing in my way, I started riding again. Everything worked out great and I regained an important part of my life.

I discovered that I had to adjust my priorities to feel happy again, and you may need to do that, too. Eliminate unnecessary responsibilities in your life. Work on incorporating your child into *your* lifestyle instead of the other way around. If someone had given me this advice, I would have done things differently from day one.

The reason I suggest you incorporate your child into *your* lifestyle is because if you don't, the feeling of being trapped can happen throughout your child's growing years. Kyle is ten years old now and on occasion, I still feel trapped. This usually happens when I over-commit myself (to school, to baby-sitting other children, to taking Kyle to after-school activities, or to doing things for Jim). Whatever it is, I have a tendency to forget about saving any time for my own priorities and end up depressed.

It's O.K. to say no and put *your* priorities first, especially as your kids get older. You'll be happier and your relationship will be better off for it. You're the only one who can control what goes on in your life, and if you don't speak up, the tension will continue to build.

When this happens you need to share your feelings with your partner. You may not even be sure what the feelings are about, but once you start talking, the answer will come and you'll begin to relax.

Be aware that the parent trap may snap shut on your partner, too. Notice when honeybun has been quieter than usual and nothing between the two of you has caused it (nothing that *you know of*, at least). Ask what's going on. Sometimes, that silence can be a sure sign the enjoyment has gone out of your partner's life. And as I said before, we don't always know the reasons behind our feelings. If you ask and the response is, "Nothing's wrong," or "I don't know," don't push for an answer. Just let your sweetheart know you're there when needed. Then share a great big "I love you like a goofball" hug.

When we choose to remain silent we stay in our heads, and our imaginations can run wild. Staying there for too long can convince us we *are* trapped. Always remember, if we were truly trapped we wouldn't be able to move or to change things.

Keep the perspective that being trapped is just a feeling and feelings can be changed. Be willing to take whatever action you need to help yourself feel free again. Freedom brings happiness. Ask anyone who's been trapped.

> *"The truth frees you. Speak your truth, and experience your freedom."*
> Linda Salazar

EXERCISE:
1. Write down what activities are missing in your life that you'd like to start doing again.

2. Share your list with your partner and make a plan to implement your desires.

~4~

Magical Moments

*"You need not be together physically
to stay connected emotionally"*
Linda Salazar

So, now you're a parent! If you're not interested in creating magical moments in your relationship then don't read another word.

Ah hah! Just as I suspected. You *are* interested. Is that because you want to feel connected to your partner or is it just that you need to feel more loved? Are you looking for more attention? What did you say? You want all this, but there's not enough time in the day for such fantasies? Bite your tongue! Have you forgotten who's writing this book? With a wave of my magic Mac keyboard, anything is possible.

Besides, I never said anything about sitting down and having a heart-to-heart conversation or spending hours at a time together. After all, that's what you don't have time for, remember? (Not in this chapter, at least.)

What I'm talking about is making time for the smallest acts of kindness—the thoughtfulness that makes you smile, that leaves you with a warm, fuzzy feeling. C'mon, stop playing with me; you know what I mean. It's that marvelous feeling that assures you that your cuddly bear is the most unique partner in the world!

Most of you did things like I'm referring to before you were parents, and if you're really fortunate, you're still doing these things. So what are they, already? Well, let me give you some ideas.

For instance: leaving love notes. "Where?" you ask. Boy, are you out of practice. Anywhere! On the bathroom mirror, bedroom mirror, pillow, in the car, briefcase, lunch, wallet, underwear drawer, even the e-mail.

Now you want to know when? Geeze! Any chance you get! It's important to let our partners know how much we appreciate them with written words. Why? Because expressing our love on paper allows them to relive those feelings every time they read our words.

Another suggestion: call your honey from work just because you're thinking about her. Hint: don't ask about the kids. Tell her you miss her and hope she's having a good day. Loving thoughts can pop into your head very quickly and as quickly as they enter, *Poof!* They're gone. You need to act on these impulses or you'll miss the boat. Don't second guess yourself. Act on your heart's desire and make the call! Don't come home and say, "Darling, I thought about calling you today to tell you how much I missed you, but I didn't have the time. Anyway, I *did* think about you." Trust me, something gets lost in the translation (such as your chances for getting a few points out of this exchange).

Now, if your thought is, "Every time I call home I get bombarded with all the turmoil that's going on; then Martha wants to know when I'll be home so she can have a break. I hate that." Fear not. I'm about to solve that issue for you with yet another touch of my magic Mac. *The person who is receiving the call should not complain in any way, shape, or form*—no matter what's going on at the time. (The exception, of course, is if Junior is dying, but be sure he's not faking it. You know how kids can be when they're vying for attention.) Instead of complaining, listen to what your partner is saying and respond appropriately. When your loved one tells you, "I was just thinking about you and I miss you," he or she is trying to connect. Be grateful. If you're not used to a call like this, don't panic. Assume your friendly caller read this section of the book and add some sentimental declarations of your own.

What do you do if you're not feeling very impassioned? *Fake it!* For the love of God, *fake it!* O.K., maybe faking it is not the best thing to do. For the sake of your relationship, at least be appreciative of your partner's effort. Your response can be, "It's crazy around here right now and your call is just what I needed to make me feel cared for. I can't wait for you to get home so we can spend some quiet time together." Chances are your partner will come home earlier than normal and help get those kids to bed ASAP.

Something tells me you're laughing at that last paragraph and moaning, "That'll never happen. Who's writing this dribble. Up to now, I thought she knew what she was talking about." It's O.K., I'm not hurt by your temporary lack of confidence. I understand. It's normal to have such thoughts when you're challenged with something new (especially if you're a parent with sleep deprivation). However, I'm asking you to stretch a little and change your automatic responses. Step outside your comfort zone. What have you got to lose? (Maybe some old attitudes.)

I shared this phone idea with the parents in one of my seminars and a gutsy husband took on the challenge. The response he received when he called his wife was hysterically funny. Calling from work one day, he told her he couldn't wait to have some time alone with her (along with some other comments that I can't mention in a G-rated book) because it had been too long. She was so stunned by the call, that she hung up on him—she thought he was a crank caller. He immediately called back, acknowledged her by name, and said, "this is your husband and so was the caller before!" It's been two years since that incident and they still laugh about it.

So, don't worry if your partner hangs up on you the first time or even the second. If at first you don't succeed, keep a sense of humor about it. Hey, it works just as well when calling from home to connect with your partner at work.

What do you do when you're both at home and it's the magic hour? You know, the time when you're trying to get dinner ready and the kids are running around with nuclear energy. The phone's ringing (it's usually from someone who wants to sell you the latest parenting magazine) and you're at your wits end after a nonstop day. Take a moment to breathe deeply, go find your significant other amongst the chaos and give a rejuvenating bear-with-it hug. If you're asked what that was for, simply say, "It's because I wanted to connect with you and because we could both use a little boost."

You're not laughing again, are you? Get hold of yourself because there's more. Throw your partner a quick glance that says, "Even though it's crazy right now everything's O.K. because we have each other." (You may have to practice that look in the mirror so you don't get escorted off to the mom-and-pop loony farm.) When you walk by your mate, give a quick peck on the cheek, with a pinch of "I wuv you, buttercup." (Hey, you're parents now, how else do you expect to talk!)

If you really feel wild, while he's shaving, drying his hair, or brushing his teeth, give him a spoon hug. (A hug from behind. Fork hugs are considerably more dangerous.) When he asks why, you say, "I just felt like it, because you're the best."

Thank yous and compliments are very important. And what's even more helpful is when you're specific about your remarks. What if you change, "Thanks for doing a great job with our son or daughter" to "You're so great when it comes to calming Rocky down. Thank you." Or to, "I really appreciate how patient you were with Adrienne when you taught her how to ride her bike."

If you haven't been able to connect all day, before

you fall asleep at night, take turns sharing one reason why you love each other. (I recommend doing this even if you can't remember why.) Then cuddle up and say, "Sweet dreams, lover."

Specifics let our partners know that we're noticing what they're doing and that we appreciate them. Even better, *they'll* appreciate *us* for the acknowledgment. It's a win/win situation. (I admit it, I'm a win/win junkie.)

Mom, what would happen if *you* bought *Dad* some flowers? I did that for my husband, only to find him moved to tears. He told me that was the first time a woman ever gave him flowers. We had been married seven years! The only regret I had at that moment was that I did this after we had a fight. As touched as he was, I wished I had done it for no reason at all.

As I've already shown you with the phone call story, not all thoughtful plans go smoothly and my next plan was no exception. When Jim went out of town on a job, I sent an arrangement of flowers to his hotel room, for no reason at all. They were to be in his room before he got back from work. Well, the night came and went without a call. The next morning I was hurt and angry. I called the hotel and sure enough the flowers had been delivered. The whole day went by and still no phone call. Finally, that evening, Jim called and told me he had gotten food poisoning the day before. He had been in the hospital for several hours before he went back to his room to sleep the rest of the day away. I was somewhat sympathetic, but wanted to know why he hadn't mentioned my sweet gesture. Ready to explode, I said in my most sarcastic voice, "I hope you're enjoying the flowers I sent you." Silence on the other end. "Jim?"

"Those flowers are from you?"

"How many other women send you flowers with a card saying 'I miss you and love you'?" I asked. As it turned out, he hadn't even read the card. He thought they came from the crew he was working with. You know the old saying, "baby poop happens."

In spite of the mishap, our special connection was achieved, thousands of miles apart, and we had a good laugh as an added bonus. By the way, shared laughter is a guaranteed way to feel close to each other, no matter how many miles apart you may be.

All the ideas I've suggested in this chapter can be implemented almost anywhere, anytime. It only takes a minute to remember you're a vital part of each other's lives.

As I was finishing up this chapter, Jim called. He thanked me for making him a sandwich to take in the car and told me how much he appreciated me. The call took all of thirty seconds and made my entire day. That is the kind of connection I'm talking about. Never stop appreciating each other—especially for the little things!

Sometimes actions speak louder than words. So use your actions to show your partner how glad you are that he or she is in your life. Your written word is very powerful and can last an eternity. Go on, take a risk and bring a smile or a tear of happiness to your sweetheart. Reveal your true essense in an instant.

The truth is:
"Those who laugh...last!"
Chinese Proverb

EXERCISE:
1. Make a list of all the things you can do to create some magical moments between you and your partner.

2. Don't tell your partner, just do the things on the list!

~5~

Who's Got the Time!

"Attention energizes, and intention transforms. Whatever you put your attention on in your life will grow stronger."
Deepak Chopra
The Seven Spiritual Laws of Success

I've got it! I've got the perfect way for you to end your relationship after you have children. If you follow my advice I guarantee success at destroying everything you've dreamed of. It's worked for thousands of other couples over the years and do you know the best part of all? It doesn't matter if you continue living together or not, your relationship will still be over. Ready? Here it is:

*Don't spend any time together and
focus all your attention on the children.*

Is that brilliant or what? Does this advice sound good to you? I hope not. Couples don't usually have children with the intention of ruining their relationship. Yet with a click of baby shoes, yesterday's gone and there's no assurance we'll have tomorrow. If we don't spend time together *today*, when will we?

Every parent knows that the most precious commodity we have is time, and thinking you don't have time for each other is phooey. That's right, *phooey*. It's a word that any human being can learn very quickly. I'm not interested in making you work at understanding what I'm telling you. Phooey means phooey. If you *want* to be together you'll *make* it happen. Let me share a couple of stories that illustrate how true this is.

It's 11:30 P.M. and I'm just getting home from a fifteen-hour work day. Dragging myself up the stairs, I notice my bedroom light is on. Oh no, I can't believe Jim's still awake. All I want to do is fall into bed and pass out. Hesitantly, I enter the room. What I see terrifies me. Not only is he awake, but he's folding laundry! Now what do I do? I decide to stay calm, pretending I don't notice anything. "Hi, honey, why are you awake and folding laundry at this hour?" (So much for not noticing.) Flashing his contagious smile, Jim says, "I'm waiting up for you because I want to spend some time together. Great, I think. Just what I need—a husband who wants to be with me after I've just worked fifteen hours. (The truth is, for the past week we've been like two minivans passing in the driveway.)

I walk over to Jim, give him a wifey kind of kiss and make sure he knows how tired I am. Unfortunately for me, his sweetness instantly has me not only chatting with him, but helping him fold the laundry. (How dare he be so sweet.) Next thing I know, he excuses himself from the room. Now that takes nerve. Here I stand, alone, amongst a bunch of unfolded sheets and pillow cases. Just as I'm about to toss the laundry aside in frustration, Jim comes back.

He's carrying a glass of water with no ice, (the way I like it), a glass of club soda for himself, two napkins and my favorite chocolate, chocolate chip cookies from Trader Joe's. As I eye him suspiciously, Jim places the drinks and food on the floor and gently takes my hand to sit me down next to him. He looks tenderly into my bloodshot eyes and says, "I do miss us and thought a midnight picnic would be a nice way to catch up with our lives." I am so touched by my husband's love for me that I melt into his embrace. For over an hour, we talk and laugh about our past week. My exhaustion turns into elation and I'm thankful I married this man and had a child with him.

The next morning, when the alarm screamed at 6:00 A.M., I wasn't the least bit tired. As a matter of fact, I slept more soundly in Jim's arms that night than I had in weeks. We didn't get to see much of each other for another week but our midnight picnic carried us through. We *took time* to be together.

This next story comes from a mother I interviewed. She and her husband (I'll call them Jack and Jill) have three kids ages one, four, and seven. Here is a perfect example that proves a canceled night out together can become a passionate night at home. This mom's imagination worked miracles.

Jack and Jill had plans to go out for a very special evening. They made reservations at the restaurant they went to on their first date and then they planned to go dancing at the nightclub where they first met. As luck would have it, the baby-sitter called in sick on the morning of their date. For hours, Jill frantically looked for a replacement and came up empty-handed. Much to her credit, instead of striking out with this setback, she stepped up to the plate and hit a home run. She called the restaurant and explained her dilemma to the manager. Then she asked if someone would deliver the meal to her house so she could serve it at home. No problem.

When Jack came home she explained what had happened and told him not to worry, "I've got something planned for us, right here." Jill asked her husband if he would put the kids down for the evening and then dress as though they were still going out.

With the kids sound asleep, Jack came back downstairs all dressed up with nowhere to go—or so he thought. By now, his home had been transformed. Jill, who was also dressed up by this time, had created a table setting as beautiful as one in their favorite restaurant. The lights were low, the candles were glowing and she took his hand as they sat down to a romantic and delicious meal. Two luxurious hours later, dinner was over.

Jill sauntered over to the CD player and put on music much like they would have danced to had they gone out. For the next hour and a half they danced and talked the night away.

During my interview with Jack, he told me it was the most endearing and intimate evening he had ever spent with his wife. He realized that night how lucky he was to have Jill in his life and how good he felt having their three kids safe and sound upstairs while Mom and Dad fell in love all over again downstairs.

So, as you can see, if you make the effort you *can* have time together. One hour can feel like all the time in the world when your two hearts connect.

Frequently, a couple will tell me they're on a tight budget. They can't afford to go out. Phooey again.

Did you see the movie, *The World According to Garp*, with Robin Williams? Well, in one scene he and his wife are going out for the evening. They hire a new babysitter and are a little nervous about leaving the kids.

When they get into the car, they see the kids and the sitter in the house, through the large living room window, having a great time. Mom and Dad decide to stay put, hold hands, talk, and watch the kids play. These parents never leave their own driveway and have a wonderful evening. Now that's an inexpensive date!

There are all sorts of ways to be together without spending a lot of money. Go for a drive. Park somewhere beautiful and talk—or whatever else suits your fancy. (Remember, this *is* a G-rated book.) Take a bikeride in your neighborhood. Go for a long walk. Plan a picnic lunch or dinner. Not every date has to be restaurants and movies. If you've got parents or friends nearby that can watch your kids, you won't have to spend any money for a sitter. Be imaginative. Get out of your everyday thinking.

The parents I talked with who had regular dates with each other, felt better about their relationship than those who didn't. Now that sounds pretty obvious, doesn't it? Well, *if it's so obvious why aren't more parents having regular date times together?* The fact is, I talked to more couples that don't make dates with each other than those that do—and in the next sentence they said they really should start to commit the time to each other.

I know that you parents have a lot going on in your lives, and I also know that if you don't do something as a couple soon, you'll end up in a rut and not do anything at all. *Somebody* has to take the stroller by the handles and start pushing.

All too often I hear parents say the following:

"I'm always the one making the plans to be together. I wish she would initiate something for a change."

"It seems as though I'm just forcing him to go out when he really doesn't want to. What fun is that?"

"When I ask her what she wants to do, her response is, 'I don't care'."

"Sometimes he forgets we have a date. Then I'm really upset and the whole evening's ruined."

I could go on and on but I'm getting bored with this. If you want to keep focusing on the negatives, be my guest. That way you can become more irritated with each other and have a legitimate reason not to be together. If you *are* the one making all the plans, so what? If you enjoy yourselves once you're out, that's what matters.

Sometimes, it helps to make plans that interest your loved one more than yourself—especially if sugarpuss has dropped hints that you should come along on some of these excursions. The point I'm making is: it's good to get the focus off yourself and put it on your partner once in awhile.

Dad, what if Mom loves to shop and you offer to go shopping with her one day? Mom, what if Dad enjoys going to sporting events and you buy tickets for the two of you? Forgive me for stereotyping, but I want to keep this simple. When you initiate this kind of action, you're saying you do care about life outside of parenting and you want your sweetheart to be happy.

Let's talk about the partner who forgets you have a date. Find someone else to go out with! Just kidding. If you know your honey forgets easily, do this: the day before, or the morning of, leave a loving reminder note. You could even drop a card in the mail telling him or her how much you're looking forward to being together. It's wonderfully effective and the best part is, you're not nagging. (Hallelujah!) One woman told me that her husband really looks forward to her reminders, and he keeps all of her notes. Whether she is worried about him remembering or not, she still continues to write the notes because they mean so much to him! (Wouldn't you just love to read what was in some of those notes?)

Too many couples I've talked with wait six months to a year to go out after having children. That's too long! The sooner you date on a regular basis, the better off everyone will be. Now, I know some of you are thinking, "But we don't have anyone we can trust with our children. We don't have any relatives nearby." Phooey, phooey, phooey! Quit whining and start networking. Talk to other parents. The only way you get results is by taking action. If you put in just a little effort you'll find someone.

If you want to test a sitter's competence, you can do trial runs. Bring the sitter in for an hour or so during the daytime. Come and go from the house with no warning. I did this with my first sitter when Kyle was three months old. I would leave the house, then come home and look in the window to see how everything was going. I also told the sitter I'd be gone for three hours and then came back in one. I had my neighbor come over and pretend she needed to see me. Sneaky? You bet. Proud of it? Absolutely. It's my child's life, and doing this enabled me to have confidence in my sitter so I could enjoy being out with my husband.

If you have unrealistically high expectations about your first date as parents, you can end up disappointed, so be careful. Two months after Kyle was born, Jim and I were finally breaking out. (That's breaking *out*, not breaking *up*.) We were so excited that you'd think Jim just got his drivers license and my parents said I could go cruising with him. As it turned out we went to dinner and all we did was talk about Kyle. We worried about him getting to sleep, taking his bottle, missing us—you name it, we worried about it. On top of that, dinner was pretty bad. When we left the restaurant, we wondered what to do next. It was too late for a movie but we had only been gone for an hour. How could we possibly go home already! There we were, our big night out—all dressed up with nowhere to go. The idea of just cruising around wasn't as exciting as it had been when we were seventeen. We looked at each other, smiled knowingly, and headed home.

Even though it had been hard for us to relax that first time out, we continued to go on dates. The more we did, the better we became at it.

If one partner is especially concerned about leaving the baby, then make plans to go out for only an hour. Be patient. Remember, this is all new and there's going to be an adjustment period.

It's not unusual when parents go away together without their children to have moments of tension. A couple in my seminar, whom I'll call Harry and Sally, shared an experience with me about their first weekend away from their daughter. They went to San Francisco for a romantic weekend and ended up fighting, instead.

One balmy evening, as they sat by the bay taking in the beauty of the city lights dancing on the water, Harry put his arm around Sally. He leaned in close and whispered something sweet to her. Her response was, "I miss our daughter so much, I wonder if she misses us, too." Harry was astounded! He jerked his arm off his wife's back and asked if she had heard what he just said. She said she hadn't and continued to talk about their daughter. After a few minutes, he blew up and started yelling about how tired he was of trying to be loving and passionate when all she could think about was the baby. Then Sally became irrational because she couldn't believe Harry *wasn't* thinking about their daughter. Get the picture?

All he wanted was his lover back for a little while. He wasn't asking her to move their daughter to the doghouse. He just thought some time away would help them reconnect. When he told her calmly how he felt, she realized what she had done and was sorry for her lack of consideration. When Sally finally turned the baby monitor off, she and Harry were able to spend their last day together like a couple of newlyweds.

Be willing to express your feelings without blame. Mom, when you're away with your partner and he's trying to renew your love, pay attention. If you're experiencing the pangs of motherhood, mention it and get over it before he starts "panging" you. And Dad, understand that the connection between Mom and her baby can be overwhelming. It doesn't mean she loves *you* any less. Get her attention back by first acknowledging how she feels. Then remind her that your time together is short and you want to make the most of it. Practice, practice, practice, have patience, patience, patience and above all, don't give up.

Never forget, time is of the essence because you *don't* know if you'll be around tomorrow to have special moments together. Look at your priorities and slow yourselves down. What good is all that hard work and money if there's no one around to share it with?

> *"Too many relationships end up as two lonely parallel lines that are always even but are never moving or touching."*
>
> Thomas Patrick Malone & Patrick Thomas Malone
> *The Art Of Intimacy*

EXERCISE:
1. Write down as many fun things to do with your partner as you can think of. Remember to include things your partner enjoys doing.

2. Put a possible calendar date next to each date idea. Create a list of possible baby-sitters. (This includes trading time with friends. Don't make any judgments.)

~6~

I Need, You Need; Now What?

> "It's a mistake to think children can't take care of themselves but a marriage can. Just as we nurture our children we must nurture ourselves."
>
> Anne Mayer
> *How to Stay Lovers While Raising Our Children*

I need sleep, I need five minutes to take a shower, I need to do the dishes, I need to clean the house, I need to do the laundry, I need to cook dinner, I need to go to the store, I need a gorilla. (I just threw that in there to see if you were paying attention.) Anyway, does this sound familiar?

These are basic needs. This is the stuff we do to get us through our daily lives; but these needs don't nurture our souls. In order to be effective parents and loving partners we absolutely need to take care of more than our basic physical needs. And that, my friends, is the purpose of this chapter: to encourage parents to take care of themselves.

After children, you may discover that you both have new needs and that the old ones require more attention. For instance: before I had Kyle, I loved socializing. Much to my surprise, when I became a mom, I longed for *a lot* of time alone. Considering that I barely read more than a newspaper pre-baby, I was astonished when reading became a passion for me and now I've written a book!

Although I knew what *I* needed, I wondered if other parents had developed strong new needs as well. So during my interviews, I asked the men and women about this. I learned that both parents discovered very definite needs that they didn't have before they had kids.

Here's what came up for the women: (Men, pay close attention; you never know what you'll learn.)

The most common need expressed by the women was the need for time alone. They all communicated how precious their down time was and that they wanted their partner to respect this time. They needed absolute peace and quiet for at least twenty minutes. (Twenty minutes? I would have gone for an hour, minimum. C'mon gals, if you're going to ask for something, ask for something!) Moving right along.

Many women needed to know that after giving birth, they were still attractive to their men.

Stay-at-home-moms who had given up their careers needed to be told they were doing great jobs. A good number of these women, myself included, thought they weren't accomplishing anything in the first few months; this belief can send a new mom spiraling into a major depression.

Also high on their list was needing less affection from their partners. I'll include myself in that one, too. (Hey, it's my book. I can if I want to.) Having a child on you all day can definitely take away the need to be touched any more than necessary. You may feel like saying, "Please don't touch me for at least five minutes!" Can this cause friction between partners? Absolutely, and I'll talk about this in detail later in the chapter.

Because babies require so much of mother's attention,

Parents In Love

the women expressed the need for their mates to fend for themselves, to be more self-sufficient.

So, there you have it. The mom's most common needs. Now it's the dad's turn. Ladies, I'll give you the same advice I gave the men: listen closely, you never know what you might learn.

Drum roll please. Number one on the list is . . . SEX. Your men need more sex! What's wrong with you women? Get to work. (I should talk.) Just so I don't get in trouble with these men, they did say they understood the situation and believed the sex would increase in time.

Girls, the next need is a big one. As a matter of fact, I have to put it right up there with sex. They need you to greet them with a good attitude when they come home from work. So many men said they were tired of coming home wondering if it was their lovers or complainers waiting for them. No matter what's going on, they really need a kiss on the lips and a hug when they enter the house. (Preferably from you.)

A lot of men need to do things their way when they take care of the baby. They're tired of being corrected when they do something different than the women.

Guess what? They also need to be acknowledged for their contribution to the family, and just like the moms, the dads need more private time. They made it very clear to me that work does not count as time to themselves. (*I* made it very clear to *them* they were wrong. I'm going to get in a lot of trouble if I don't stop this nonsense.)

One last need that was mentioned, which I personally appreciated, was the need for more mutual respect. That should make you moms feel good.

I'm sure there are plenty of needs you may have that weren't mentioned here. However, for the parents I spoke to, those were the winners. Let's talk about a few of them.

As I said, we women need less physical affection than we did before we had children. This can cause a lot of problems between couples. To this day, I still don't need as much affection as I did before motherhood.

Our lovers can feel hurt when we don't physically need them as much as we did before. To make matters worse, dads tend to need *more* affection because so much is given to the baby and taken away from them. So what do we do? We tell them to grow up or hit the road. No, no. I'm just kidding. We find a middle ground. We respect each other's needs.

Mom, you can say something like this to your partner, "Get your grimy hands off of me, you pig!" (There I go again! I'm really sorry.) O.K., I'll try one more time. How about this? "Honey, the kids have been on me all day and I could really use twenty minutes without anyone touching me. After that, I'll be able to give you the attention and affection *you* need." When you do this, you're very specific about *your* need, your partner won't feel unwanted, and he is reassured that his needs will get met.

If he wants a hug because he hasn't seen you all day, I suggest you go ahead and hug him so he knows you're glad to see him.

To be alone is important for both men and women. Kids fill up our days so completely that it's hard to find one second to ourselves, let alone an hour. Nonetheless, finding the time is a necessity.

So how do you do this without your sweetheart feeling

cheated out of his or her quiet moments? First of all, ask for time *before* your fuse blows. All too often, one parent will be on the edge of a cliff ready to jump, but not say a word, and then suddenly blurt out, "I've been with these kids all day and if I don't get to be alone soon I'll kill you and then myself." I don't know, call me crazy, but my intuition tells me it's best if you ask *before* you get to that point.

Here's an alternative that's not so violent and there's no mess to clean up. Say, "I know you've been working long hours all week and I'm ready for a break from the kids. Let's figure out a plan so you get to relax and feel rejuvenated and I can get some time to myself, as well." Now you've acknowledged your partners' needs along with your needs and you've negotiated for a win/win.

Sometimes one parent is at the end of his rope and the other parent has lots of energy. Without being asked, the parent who has the energy should offer the other person a break. You'll be greatly appreciated and I promise this act of kindness will come back to you.

No matter what your needs are, don't cop out with an attitude like, "If he can't see how much help I need or how little affection I'm getting, I'm certainly not going to ask. He should already know." Sorry, it just doesn't work that way. Here's my motto: "Ask and you shall receive, don't ask and you'll get bupkis." (If you don't know what bupkis is, don't ask for what you want and find out.)

You may have noticed or will soon notice, that as your children grow, their needs change. The same rule applies for both parents. Nothing stays the same forever and you'll find yourselves developing new needs as you drop old ones.

Over the years your personal growth will have an affect on your needs. You must be willing to adjust with one another. Just because your partner needed a lot of alone time last month doesn't mean she'll feel the same way this month. Inform each other as your needs shift. Remember, neither of you can read minds.

Needs are a very important part of who we are as human beings. Everyone has them and it's up to us to find ways to get them met. It's not our partner's fault if their needs get met and ours don't. We should stop and look at what we're not doing or saying, and take whatever action is necessary to create a change so our needs *do* get recognized.

Respect yourself enough to realize you deserve what you need and then ask in a loving way. The truth is, you really do want to have as much happiness in your life as possible. Trust your loved one enough to know that he or she wants the same for you. Go ahead, ask. Who knows, you *might* get everything you need.

>
> *"Having needs is as natural as breathing. Parents need to breathe as much as their children. Take a deep breath and get your needs met."*
> Linda Salazar

EXERCISE:
1. Write down what you need from your partner now that you're a parent. (Such as more compliments, time alone, affection.)

2. Share these needs with your partner.

3. The listening partner should repeat what he or she heard so you both know your needs are understood clearly.

4. Begin implementing ways to fulfill the needs.

~7~

Sex–What Sex?

Parenthood: "That state of being better chaperoned than you were before you were married."
Marcelene Cox,
Free-lance columnist

Are you wondering why I came up with this title? Well, maybe you're not, but I'm going to tell you anyway. During my interviews I would say, "Let's talk sex." The response from 90% of both men and women was either, "*What* sex?" or uncontrollable laughter—which I decided meant the same thing as "*What* sex?"

There's a big shift in sexual activity for most couples after children. How that shift affects these couples depends on many things: patience, understanding, communication, desire, sense of humor, level of exhaustion, self-esteem, responsibilities, current cellulite status—you name it, and it will make a difference in their sex lives, either positive or negative.

After I had Kyle, I struggled a great deal, sexually. O.K., let's be honest here: after having Kyle, the thought of sex was about as appealing as being nine centimeters dilated before the epidural. On the other hand, my husband was ready for action way before our holding period was up.

When I went back to the doctor for my six-week checkup, I cringed when I heard her words, "Have at him." Have at him? Was she nuts? I felt like saying, "If you're so excited about it, *you* have at him." I begged for more time. I bribed her. I offered her money *and* my baby. Anything to keep me from having to do the inevitable.

Every desire to be intimate with my husband in that way had been exorcised from my soul. For the first time, celibacy sounded very enticing. I *could* become celibate. I could write a bestseller with the title, *The Fastest Way to Celibacy: Have a Baby.*

There was just one hitch—I wasn't the only party involved here. In a marriage it takes two to agree to celibacy just as it takes two to have a baby. Much to my dismay, I couldn't convince my husband how much fun we would have if we stayed out of each others' skivvies. (After three years without sex who could blame him? I'm kidding. It wasn't three years. It was two years and eleven months.) All right, all right already, none of that's true. I'm not sure how long it was, perhaps a few weeks after my six-week checkup. But I am sure if Jim were writing this book he could be more specific. Anyway, what I do know is that I was a tough mom to crack; my legs were permanently crossed, and the idea of sex was a galaxy away.

Between exhaustion, having a baby on me all day, and the unceasing demands of motherhood, I'm amazed I can say we became sexually active again before long. I will admit, however, that it's never been the same as it was before we had Kyle. The spontaneity, the frequency, my desire, have all changed. Has this been a problem? No. But it could have been if we had not been willing to

Parents In Love

talk about what *had* changed.

Once in a while, some couples will tell me their sex lives are better since having children. They look me straight in the eye and claim they have no problems. Liars. O.K., maybe they're not liars, but the heck with them. I'm going to concentrate on the 99.9% of the people who told me about all their struggles with sex after children. (It makes for a juicier chapter.)

Seriously, most parents go through rough times because sex does take a back seat after a baby is born. For how long? That depends on the parents. For the first couple of months, it's fairly common that both partners are so tired they hardly notice the other one exists, at least as far as sex is concerned. But once the sleep deprivation subsides, one of you (and yes, dads, you're usually that one) will get the urge to move from the back seat and get behind the wheel. Now the challenge is to get your erstwhile lover into the front seat with you. But when your honeybunch is stuck in park, you've got a problem. Now you need to work on the situation so you *can* get your sex life into gear.

There's no question that men and women have different perspectives about sex. This is well expressed in the Woody Allen movie, *Annie Hall.* Picture this: Woody's in a session with his therapist. The therapist asks him how often he and his wife (Diane Keaton) are having sex. Woody says, "We're hardly having sex at all, maybe three or four times a week." Cut to Diane Keaton with her therapist who asks the same question. Diane's response, "All the time, about three or four times a week." And they didn't even have a child!

So what do you do about this dilemma?

You exercise patience and communicate with each

other so you understand what stage you're in with your sexual desire. You learn the art of compromise. You know full well that marriage relationships can't survive without some sexual activity unless, of course, both parties agree to celibacy. (Speaking from experience, chances of that range from slim-to-forget it.) Learn to be more creative with your intimate time and stop comparing your sex life to the way it was before kids.

Ladies, you need to be completely open with your men. (No, no! Not that kind of open!) What I mean is, if you don't seem to have desire at all, let them know how they can help. Considering what emotional and physical changes women go through after having babies, it's a miracle couples have more than one child.

As mentioned before, many of the women revealed that the constant love and touching from their babies lessened their need for physical intimacy from their partners. This may be acceptable for a certain period of time, but your partner may soon begin to feel rejected and hurt. Together, you need to build a new bridge that will bring back the intimacy in your lives—much like the bridge you built to expand your relationship in the beginning stage.

When you first started dating you wanted to know all about your new cuddly bear—what kind of childhood he had, what his beliefs and values were, what made him feel loved. You even wanted to know what turned him on and got his mojo movin'. Well, guess what? It's time to find out what gets each other's mojos on the prowl, again.

Be inquisitive. With the abundant changes you've gone through, the sexual desires you had before parenthood may not be the same now. You need to ask each other, "What's changed for you, sexually? What do you need from me now?" When you ask these questions it shows you care enough to regain the intimacy that will bring the two of you back together.

I can't stress enough the importance of being completely honest and open with each other. (I hope we're clear on the kind of open I'm referring to.) Talking about sex may be uncomfortable for one or both of you. Nonetheless, it must happen. Without talking, you can't build that bridge. You end up on opposite sides of the chasm with no way to reach each other.

Ladies, if you're going through some of the emotional turmoil I talked about in the "Who Am I?" chapter, it's time to speak up. Those kinds of personal changes will have a large effect on your sex drive. Your men need to know what's going on. The only way they can begin to understand, accept, and help is by your willingness to share. It also lets your partners know that your lack of desire has nothing to do with them; understanding that fact can make a huge difference in all areas of your relationship.

If you're not feeling sexy or attractive, say so. Chances are, your partner doesn't see you as you see yourself and may even find you *more* attractive now that you're the mother of his child. I'll let you in on a little secret; the majority of men I spoke with told me that they found their women much more alluring since childbirth. (Don't let on I told you that.) Let him help you find your way back to feeling sexy again. Who knows? It might be fun.

However, I've come to understand that it's not only the women's desire for sex that can drop. Some men expressed that suddenly seeing their ladies as the mother of their children more than their lovers made it difficult to become aroused. If this rings true for some of you dads, share that with your partner. She needs to know that your lack of interest is not about her being unattractive—especially if she has already told you she feels unattractive.

Other men had the opposite experience. They said that their sexual propensity increased so much that it had a negative impact on their relationships. Because the moms were so busy with the babies, the dads began to feel unloved, needing a sexual outlet to *be* loved. They desperately wanted to connect with their partners. Remembering how their past romantic overtures lit a fire before parenthood, they tried the same approach after parenthood, but with little success. Unfortunately, when the men were pushy and didn't explain their needs or desires, the women became very upset with them. This led to some serious tension and the dads felt even more rejected and frustrated.

When a situation elicits this kind of misunderstanding, it's critical that you explain the reasons behind your actions and feelings. Talking about the issues gives you the tools to build bridges and cultivate compassion and patience.

Physical and emotional changes are not all that keeps parents from being lovers again. Once your child reaches about two years of age and older, some interesting circumstances can develop. The idea of a little person walking in on you can certainly curtail your desire for intimacy. I'm here to tell you it's not the end of the world if they *do* walk in on you and children's curiosity can make for very humorous moments.

As crazy as this may sound, there was one morning

when Jim and I were actually *both* in the mood. We thought Kyle was still asleep and wouldn't be up for another half hour or so. We decided to go for it! Well, much to our surprise, in the middle of our activity, we heard a little three-year-old voice: "Hi, Mommy and Daddy. What are you doing?" Talk about being caught in the act! Luckily, my mind kept working even though my body froze. Quickly, I responded with, "I'm just trying to get comfortable." (Hah! Now there's an understatement.) I rolled off Jim and continued to squirm around "trying to get comfortable." As Kyle climbed into bed with us, he asked, "Are you comfortable now, Mommy?" (I didn't bother to answer.) For about fifteen minutes, the three of us talked and had fun. When the fun wore off for Kyle, he decided to go play in his room. Jim and I had a huge laugh about the incident and we even had the nerve to take up where we left off.

Keeping your humor is the key to a healthy sexual relationship; and it doesn't hurt to remain calm when unforeseen circumstances arise. We could have been mortified, choosing to avoid sex unless Kyle wasn't home. If we had done that, our score would have dropped to zero.

This story illustrates that for parents, having leisurely sex anytime you want can be detrimental to your health, especially if you have weak hearts. To become nostalgic about the way it was before children won't do you any good, either. If anything, that can bring on more stress and frustration, which is even worse for your health.

Work from the present moment; take advantage of any window of opportunity you may have. The feeling that you're getting away with something is a great way to put a little excitement back into your sex life. (Even if you do get caught, the excitement's still there—it's just a different kind of excitement.)

Learn to be flexible. If the window of opportunity presents itself but you're not in the mood, go for it anyway. You may be very surprised how "in the mood" you can become. Warning: *If you always wait to be in the mood, you'll never have sex again.*

After you have kids, exhaustion is an ongoing reality. So guess what that means? You now have a permanent excuse for never having sex ever again. (Who am I kidding?) There are going to be times that no matter how tired you feel, you need to take the plunge. If several weeks, a month, or even a year passes by without sex, and sweet face is hinting around for some, it's not appropriate to keep saying how tired you are. Your come-hither baby is probably tired too, but still wants to connect with you intimately. You're better off in the long run to occasionally ignore your exhaustion and give it the old college try. Chances are, you'll enjoy yourself more than you thought you would and sleep more soundly.

Before I close this chapter, I want to leave you with three words: "your well-being." The better you feel about yourself emotionally, physically, and spiritually, the better your sex life will be. You absolutely must take care of yourself. You'll have more energy and you'll have more of a desire to give of yourself when you don't believe you're constantly being taken *from.* I've said it before and I'll say it again. Find the time and ask for the time to care for yourself. Besides, when you both realize that your desire for sex is directly related to your well-being, your honey bunch will make sure you keep your engine tuned. Before you know it, you'll be going on some long drives together.

> *"Staying in touch by surprising each other with thoughtful gestures, and being considerate of one anothers needs, goes a long way toward creating the desire for sex."*
>
> Anne Mayer
> *How to Stay Lovers While Raising Children*

EXERCISE:
1. Write down any desires that have changed for you, sexually. Do you need more or less of something? Do you need new ways to put you in the mood? Are you concerned about the frequency? Too much, too little? Don't hold back; write it all down.

2. After one partner has shared, discuss the issues and begin finding ways to create what is necessary to get your sex life back into drive. When that partner feels complete with the discussion, start with number one on the other partner's list and discuss his or her issues. (This exercise could take at least an hour, so you may want to write your thoughts down beforehand, then set a time to sit and discuss them.)

~8~

Talk To Me; I'm Listening

"There are problems in all relationships. The greatest sign of love is being able to work them out."
David Viscott
I Love You, Let's Work It Out

I'm standing in the kitchen vigorously mashing away at boiled Idaho potatoes. My cheerful eighteen-month-old skips into the room. He's chatting away about something and I have no idea what he's saying. Without missing a mash, I ask, "What is it you want?" He says something that I still don't comprehend. He repeats himself once more, only this time with frustration and anger in his voice.

As I continue to pulverize the potatoes, I point to things in the kitchen asking, "Is this what you want? How about this, or this?" Kyle's so annoyed with me by now, that he's ready to split his diaper.

Not wanting the smelly mess on my floor, I come to my senses and stop mashing. I kneel down next to his two-foot frame, look directly into his big, sparkling eyes and give him my entire attention. Calmly I say, "Tell me one more time what you want." As clear as the sparkle in his eyes, he says, "I want my cookie." He's pointing up to the counter. There, sitting next to the half-mashed potatoes, is his beloved cookie. I give him the cookie along with a kiss, and off he skips as joyful as he was when he entered the kitchen.

At that moment it occurred to me that it wasn't Kyle who was unclear, it was my listening that was the problem. I was so preoccupied with my mashing that I was only half listening.

Half listening. Does this sound familiar? How many times have we half listened to our partners? Probably more than we care to admit. (Actually, since I'm writing a chapter about communication, I don't think *I'll* admit to anything.)

When Jim and I became parents, it was very clear to me that we had a lot to learn about effective communication. (That *was* an admission, wasn't it? Oh, well.) After I talked to other parents I realized we were not alone in this department.

These parents said they didn't fight very much before parenthood. But after their babies, it seemed that's all they did. They didn't know how to communicate with each other without getting upset. This is understandable.

With everything that goes on in life after parenthood, there are many more situations to bring on tension. Now that you're parents, it's vital that you talk to each other so you not only hear what is being said, but so you believe you've been heard.

Communication is an art. It's about shutting off the chatter in your head and establishing an opening so your partner's words reach your heart where authentic communication takes place. When your communications go heart-to-heart, you don't have the urge to defend yourself. In other words, you'll be able to explain your side without defensiveness.

Here's how you do this. Be aware of what you're thinking every time you and your sweetheart talk or have a disagreement. Are you really hearing her words? Are you present? Is your mind open? Are you judging what she's saying? Are you thinking how wrong he is before he even finishes his sentence? Are you preparing yourself for a response? When you notice your mind having its own conversation, just say "Stop!" Your inner silence is what allows his or her words to reach your heart.

Ask your partner to repeat herself if you miss what she says. This lets her know you care and that you want to understand. When you listen attentively, your disagreements will be resolved much more quickly, and when you have kids, every nanosecond counts.

Listening, however, is only 50% of the communication. How you express your thoughts is the other 50%. If you're upset and you say to your partner, "You never take a turn giving the kids a bath and I hate that," or, "You never help around the house. You're always finding other things to do. I'm the one doing everything around here," in this author's opinion, it will be difficult for the person listening to shut off the inner chatter. He will prepare to defend himself or shut down altogether and not hear anything beyond "you never." "Never" is a bad choice of words. (Never use "never".) Chances are, somewhere along the way, your partner *has* done what *you're claiming* he has *never* done. Even if it's once, that's not never.

Nobody likes to be yelled at, blamed, or ridiculed. And if you're at all like me, you choose your words more carefully with your kids than with your mate.

Learn to communicate with appreciation and understanding. Let's take the bath issue and try this approach on for size: "I could use a break and it would mean a lot to me if you would give the kids a bath. I know they'd love to spend the time with you and besides, according to them, I'm too boring when I give them one." You've accomplished three things here—not bad for a beginner. You didn't blame, you asked out of love and you let your partner know it would mean a lot to you and the kids. How could your lover resist? (Well, I guess anything's possible.)

When you tell each other how you feel about an issue, it's important to start with "I feel . . ." not, "you make me feel . . . ." The latter will put one of you on the defensive immediately. Take responsibility for your feelings and actions. The choice is yours and yours alone.

When you communicate to someone the way you want to be communicated to, you're ahead of the game. Here's a piece of advice that can do wonders for your relationship: *try to understand your partner first before you need to be understood.* This puts your discussions on a whole new level.

Obviously, some issues will be bigger and more heated than others. The same rules still exist; *listen* with an open heart and a clear mind. *Speak* from your heart and eliminate the blame and ridicule. Respect one another.

I know this is asking a lot when you're tired and overwhelmed. Suggestion: when you're on edge, hold back what you want to communicate if you can't say it in a productive manner. Be aware of your mood and level of patience and wait until you can think more clearly so you don't react from pure emotions. When you wait, not only does your communication become more effective, it also prevents blowups in front of your kids. By the way, if you do blow up, it isn't the end of the world. (It may be the end of the evening's peace, but not the end of the world.)

When I was a new parent, one of my biggest concerns was how Kyle was going to be affected if Jim and I had a fight in front of him. Ten years later, the words "if Jim and I" have become "whenever Jim and I." (Another admission! If I keep on at this rate, I'm not going to have any secrets left.) What I've come to learn is that it's inevitable that parents are going to fight in front of their kids. Believe it or not, this can be a healthy experience for everybody when it's handled honestly.

Kyle was about two years old when Jim and I had our first fight directly before his virgin eyes. In the middle of it he came running up to us, grabbed our hands, put them together, told us to stop, made us hug, and said, "Mommy, Daddy, love." Talk about ruining the mood. We told him to get lost. (You don't really believe that, do you?) We calmed down and immediately explained to him that fighting doesn't mean we don't love each other. We can get upset sometimes and continue to be a family.

Another time when Jim and I weren't communicating well (also known as having a fight), six-year-old Kyle was already asleep, or so we thought. In the middle of the argument we heard him crying. We both bolted upstairs, sat on his bed and held him until he calmed down. Then we told him that even though we were arguing we still loved each other very much. We said we were going back downstairs to continue talking until we worked everything out. He made us promise to come back when we resolved the problem.

That we did. This time we were smiling and holding hands and he learned that it's O.K. to argue and it doesn't mean we're going to leave each other. I have to admit, every time Kyle interrupted a fight, we were able to go back and discuss our problem calmly, so, maybe there *is* one advantage to starting a fight in front of the kids (as long as you both can be respectful).

To this day, when there's an issue that requires our urgent attention, we tell Kyle we need to step away for a few minutes to clear things up. At times, he still gets nervous when we do this, but then he remembers we always come back feeling closer to one another.

FEARS

If you find yourself with new fears after parenthood, you're not alone. Through my workshops and from talking to other parents, I've learned that many of them have had or do have fears in regard to their children; I'm talking about fears so strong that they caused monumental tension in their relationships. If this is happening to you, I recommend that you communicate these fears to your partner, immediately. To keep quiet because you're afraid of looking foolish is an indication that you don't trust your partner enough to respect your feelings and to not make fun of you. If this *is* the case, then preface your statement by saying, "I'm a little embarrassed about what I want to say, so please don't laugh or tell me I'm crazy. Just hear me out."

I want to share a story with you about a man in one of my workshops who had a fear he had hidden from his wife. During the workshop, I asked the participants to reveal to their partners a fear that they had been keeping to themselves. After about five minutes, I noticed a couple holding each other and crying.

They had just experienced a major breakthrough. The husband, whom I'll call John, told his wife, whom I'll call Joan, about his fear of their daughter being molested in preschool.

For a year, John and Joan had been looking for a preschool and John was never happy with any of the ones they investigated. No matter how great a school's reputation, he came up with reason after reason why it wasn't good enough. Joan was going crazy with this and during their year of searching, many fights erupted. The closer they got to decision time, the more they fought.

Finally, during the workshop, John had spoken his truth and the weight was lifted off his shoulders. Joan was completely sympathetic toward her husband, but she asked why he hadn't told her before now. He said he was embarrassed and felt she wouldn't understand.

Remember, your feelings are just as important as your partner's and when you hold back your feelings, for fear of hurting your partner, you're making their feelings *more* important than your own. Please don't do that. For a year, John had lived in his own hell about this issue. He caused many fights that could have been avoided if he had been authentic with his communication.

By admitting his fear out loud and receiving Joan's support, John was able to push through the fear. The following week they went out and found a preschool for their daughter.

If you've got a fear that you know is bringing stress into your relationship, speak your truth now. Be willing to be vulnerable because you can't be genuine without being vulnerable. As for the listening partner, the more you try to understand and accept your lover's feelings, the more he or she will share with you.

Fear is a strong emotion and the sooner we communicate it the sooner we can eliminate it or at least lessen its intensity. Remember this acronym for fear: False Evidence Appearing Real.

Learn from your little bundles of joy, because they exemplify authentic communication. They may need a lesson or two in tactfulness, but they can teach *us* honesty. If they've been hurt, they let us know; they make sure their feelings are heard.

We need to do the same. I'm going to repeat this important principle: if we hold back our feelings because we don't want to hurt our partners or cause them stress, then we make *their* feelings more important than *our own*. Once we do that, resentment builds up and we may take out our frustrations on the kids as well as our partners. Arguments can develop that have nothing to do with the real problem and all communication goes out the window.

This is not only unfair to the kids but to the family as a whole. We cannot grow as families if we don't communicate. It doesn't matter if it's sharing what took place during the day or expressing our deepest fear. The fact is, we need to constantly work on our communication. The more we do this, the fewer arguments we'll have; and the more we'll avoid allowing our negative feelings to build up to the point where we scream at our loved ones.

Only one issue at a time can be dealt with when communicating authentically. This means that you need to get past the anger and understand why you feel hurt—what was the circumstance that triggered your emotion. When you've accomplished this you can speak more clearly and you're not bombarding your partner with past issues with the intention to purposefully hurt him or her. Authentic communication *is* allowing yourself to be vulnerable with your feelings.

> *"True communication takes courage. It requires the willingness to take the risk of showing yourself to the other person. It is an exchange of feelings and information that can open both people to more awareness and love."*
> Daphne Rose Kingman
> True Love

EXERCISE:
1. Write down your biggest fears now that you're a parent.

2. Share these fears with your partner. The person listening should acknowledge the fear with compassion; together discuss what can be done to lessen the fear. (Do not tell your partner that there's no need to be fearful of anything he or she mentioned. That doesn't eliminate their fears.)

3. Pick one issue that's been bothering you and

share it with your partner without blame. Remember, you want to create a win/win situation.

4. Make a list of specific actions your partner does that you appreciate and read them to him or her.

5. Look into your partner's eyes and take turns reminding each other why you fell in love and why you still love each other.

~9~

Dreams Are Forever

"Dreams are the seedlings of realities."
Deepak Chopra
The Seven Laws of Spiritual Success

Think back, before you had children, when you and your lover would talk about what you wanted in your lives together: what you wanted to do . . . the places you were going to travel . . . the kind of house you would raise the kids in . . . the daring adventures you'd go on . . . where you were going to retire. Those were beautiful moments, and just because you're parents, there's no reason you can't have those moments again.

Daphne Rose Kingman, author of *True Love*, wrote, "Revealing your dreams is an act of trust. It means you believe you can share your innermost secrets and that if your aspirations turn to ashes, the person you love will still be there to comfort you."

To have this kind of trust with each other enables you to keep your spark alive. Your dreams and desires are important. They nourish the belief that the two of you share a special secret.

Your children have dreams and you do everything in your power to support and encourage them. You'll even ask probing questions just to stretch their minds. You and your partner need to do the same for each other. Dreams are not just for children. They're for everybody, and without them we're dead meat.

When you share your dreams, you put life back into your relationship. You reveal things to each other that no other person on the planet knows. You keep a part of your relationship separate from the kids. You establish an oasis that exists just for the two of you, and you escape from everything else.

You and I have been through enough by now so you know better than to tell me you don't have time for such fantasies. But just in case: lack of time is no reason to eighty-six your dreams. Discussing your dreams can be done anywhere, anytime—while you're driving, walking, eating, making dinner, relaxing in bed, flying on an airplane, talking on the phone. It can take ten minutes or ten hours. As a matter of fact, this is the easiest idea in the entire book. (For example, sharing dreams is a heckuva lot easier than being sexy when you feel about as sexy as Miss Piggy.)

I'll never forget the night Jim and I were in bed watching the news. A report came on about underprivileged kids and the volunteers who took them places they'd never been before. At that moment Jim mentioned the idea of developing a camp where less fortunate kids could learn about nature and surviving outdoors. I'd never heard this from him before and we'd been married for thirteen years! He shared a few other thoughts that truly intrigued me. I asked questions to feed his imagination. As he continued, his eyes filled with tears. A part of him had been deeply touched and I was honored to be in this experience with him. Before we knew it, an hour had gone by and a whole dream had been invented. During that hour it was just the two of us in the whole, wide world—just the two of us captured by a dream and shared feelings. This built a bond no one else will ever be a part of.

Deep down, we knew this dream wasn't something that was going to be pursued—at least not anytime soon. But that wasn't the issue; what mattered was Jim's willingness to risk sharing something with me that may have sounded completely insane. I could have shut him down with, "That's crazy; you don't have the knowledge or money to do that." A response like that is a nice way of saying, "Sorry, I'm not interested in your loony toon fantasies." If I had said that, a wall would have been erected between us and the chances of him telling me about any future dreams would be zip.

You don't want that to happen to you and your partner. Dream-sharing is an opportunity to encourage each other—to reach out and say, "I'm interested in you beyond the present moment. I'm excited about building our future together." It doesn't matter how outrageous your dreams are, and it's irrelevant if the dreams seem attainable or not. The only thing that counts is the closeness that's felt between the two of you as you inspire each other's hopes and dreams.

Sharing dreams can bring you out of your everyday routine and help you avoid boredom and depression. It's an opportunity to revitalize yourselves, to laugh again, to explore your imaginations, to believe you are the only two people on the planet. And the best part is, the dreams don't have to come true to make them an important way to be with your sweetheart on a deeper level.

I began dreaming two dreams after Kyle was born. You're reading one of them and the other was to create a workshop for parents. I didn't have a clue how to make either of them happen. But I talked to Jim about it and he asked motivating questions. Sometimes I thought I was crazy for having these dreams. Other times I knew there was no way to stop me. Through Jim's constant support and much personal perseverance, my dreams did come true.

With these accomplishments came a greater sense of self—I became a happier mother and wife. I believed then and still believe, that having Kyle enables me to dream bigger than ever before in my life. The constant support Jim and I give to Kyle to go after his dreams flows over into *our* lives. Our belief in him ultimately becomes belief in ourselves and our relationship.

The key to having our partners share their dreams is to listen with our hearts, to have the conviction that their dreams *can* happen. It also helps to ask questions to help expand on the ideas; to throw in some of our own suggestions. It's a great gift to our partners to get excited and allow their dreams to be just as they imagine them.

Don't let go of the dreams that still sit deep in your own heart. Remember, it's your dreams that brought you together; let it be your dreams that keep you together.

"Dreams are life lived on the inside without constraints of time or space or measure."
James Redfield & Carol Adrienne
Celestine Prophecy—Experiential Guide

EXERCISE:
1. Write down dreams you think about from time to time; places you want to visit, people you want to meet, careers that interest you. Stretch yourself, don't hold back. Do this for three minutes without stopping.

2. When your three minutes are up, read your dreams to your partner. You may be surprised what you learn about your sweetheart.

3. After you've both shared your dreams take turns asking questions about some of those dreams and developing them further. Have fun with this!

~10~

Words of Wisdom

"Words can heal, especially when they come from those who have been where you are."
Linda Salazar

During my interviews I asked the moms and dads, "What advice or words of wisdom would you give other parents in regard to their relationships?" All the answers I received were inspiring and insightful. When reading these parents' comments, it's apparent to me what helps them to maintain harmony in their homes.

I've selected some of my favorite quotes (not an easy decision) that support many of the issues I've talked about in the book. I have a suggestion. Don't just read them once. Continue to read them over and over until they become a part of you and you're unconsciously doing some or all of these things. By the way, if you come across advice that you think you're already following, it never hurts to be reminded to keep doing the good things you're doing.

With all that said, take a break from me and enjoy the opportunity to see what others have to say. (I hope I can manage to stay away long enough for you to read their advice uninterrupted.)

Mom's Pearls

"Keep your partner involved in everything you're doing and feeling. This will help you realize that all the changes you're going through aren't your partner's fault." — Tracy — Pasadena, Calif.

"Make it clear to your partner from the beginning what you need. Don't let issues build up. If too much time goes by after a disagreement, the incident can become bigger than it really is. Listen with your heart and acknowledge your partner's feelings." — Susan — Los Angeles, Calif.

"Don't stop communicating. Even if it's leaving notes. You don't have to be a good speaker to communicate." — Rebecca — Texas

"Both parents are equally important in a child's eyes. Therefore, both should be 100% responsible and involved." — Patsy — La Crescenta, Calif.

"If you remember to always take care of each other you can get through anything." — Amy — West Los Angeles, Calif.

"Put everything on hold the first two-and-a-half months. When you're tired you may say things you don't really mean, or your communication may be ineffective. Hold off judging the situation and each other until you've become more comfortable as parents and aren't sleep deprived." — Delilah — Dallas, Texas

"Be flexible and patient. Really work on being loving with your mate. It's so easy to get consumed by your children. When you want everything to be perfect and lovely for them it's easy to ignore your mate." — Laura — Santa Monica, Calif.

"Communicate. Don't just vent. Think about what you're going to say, especially in the first year. Remember, when you're loving your baby you need to be loving toward your partner as well. Be nurturing to each other. Go out as a couple as soon as possible and do it on a weekly basis. You should work on your relationship because of the kids." — Leslie — Van Nuys, Calif.

"The first six weeks to three months is all-consuming with the baby. After that period you should shift as much of your attention as possible back onto your partner so you don't forget what it's like to be a couple. You started out a couple and you should still be a couple when your children are grown and out of the house." — Jeanne — Saugus, Calif.

"Don't forget about each other. I found myself doing that, thinking about my baby more than my husband. That puts a lot of stress on a relationship. Keep each other's needs at the top of the list." — Amy — Santa Monica, Calif.

"Beyond one month of age your partner needs to come first. The worst thing you can do is to stop kissing because the baby started crying and is a little uncomfortable. Moms don't need to jump at every little whimper.

It's very important to teach your children how important Mommy and Daddy are to each other." — Joan — Bryan, Texas

"Always remember you're a couple. That's the most important aspect. Parents are in charge and they need to put themselves first whenever possible." — Anna — Manhattan Beach, Calif.

Hi! I know I haven't been gone that long and I'm really sorry to interrupt, but I just had to comment on the last few statements. So many parents argue with me that the kids need to come first. I'm going to clarify something here; putting you and your partner first does not mean you're neglecting the kids. It does not mean you ignore them when they're hurt, sick, or need a hug. It doesn't mean the child police are going to come and take little Buster away.

What it does mean is re-establishing a bond with your partner strong enough that you'll be able to weather any storm. The compelling love you have for each other will automatically overflow onto the kids because that's how happiness works. When you're happy with your lover, you *want* to help each other more and you *are* a better parent. You *will* have more energy and patience for everyone in the family. Remember, you don't live *for* your kids, you live *with* them.

O.K., I'm leaving you to yourself again.

"Be aware of what your partner is doing and where he is in his life. Keep the empathy for each other and know what you're both going through. Get as much sleep as possible; otherwise your perspective of what's really *going on in your relationship is thrown way off. Remain the best of friends."* — Sandy — Santa Monica, Calif.

"Keep communicating. Dropping hints about what you need doesn't work. Your partner can't read your mind. Be clear what it is you need and ask for it with kindness." — Marsha — Redondo Beach, Calif.

"Love each other and the parenting part will come. If you're attentive to your partner and their needs, you'll know when to step in and give relief." — Melanie — Palos Verdes, Calif.

"Don't try to be a super mom or dad—especially on little sleep. You can't do it all; and remember how much you're already doing just by sharing your love with your children." — Jennifer — Englewood, N.J.

"If Mom isn't happy, nobody's happy. Stay-at-home moms should get out as much as possible and let Dad take over for awhile. Take as much time for yourself as possible. You'll be a better parent and partner for it." — Sarah — Canyon Country, Calif.

"When you feel overwhelmed you must share that with your partner. Together, find ways to lessen that feeling. Eliminate some things you're doing that aren't important. You don't have to get the laundry done every day or have an immaculate house. These things can't get done the way they used to, and you should ease up on yourself." — Nancy — Los Angeles, Calif.

"My advice is for the men. If Mom is the main caretaker, help in any way you can without having to ask

her. If she's working and wants to be home with the baby, find a way to make that happen. A woman separated from her child is in stress and that makes the relationship stressful." — Cara — Provo, Utah

"Don't throw the baby at Dad when he walks in the door. He's tired, too. Give him some space before putting requests on him." — Darcy — Westwood, Calif.

O.K., I'm back, because the above quote is another hot issue. Yes, being home with a baby all day is exhausting and quite frankly can destroy most usable brain cells. (Why do you think it took me ten years to sit down and write this book? I was waiting for some of those cells to grow back.) However, slam dunking the baby into Dad's arms before he's had a chance to shut the door can leave him less than appreciative. He *is* tired and needs to breathe before jumping into another role. Give him time to unwind—ten to twenty minutes if you can stand it. Let him change clothing, shower, read the paper, whatever helps him transition out of the working world and into the home life. He'll love you for it and probably be willing to jump in more quickly when not pressured. If he doesn't show any signs of getting ready to help out, then ask, but don't ask with resentment. For a reminder of how to do this, reread the "I Need, You Need" chapter. Bye!

"Remember, dads go through emotional changes as well as moms. Being parents is hard on both people and you need to work on understanding what each parent is going through emotionally." — Andrea — San Francisco, Calif.

"Try to live in the moment as much as possible. Time goes by so quickly. Situations can seem worse than they really are. Be grateful for everything you have because parenting and having a partner to share it with is a phenomenon. Take the time to stop and enjoy it." — Karen — Newport Beach, Calif.

AMEN! (Yep, that was me again.)

Dad's Gems

"Make time for each other. Focus on what's important to the two of you. Do things that improve yourself as a person, partner and father." — Rick — Santa Monica, Calif.

"Don't let your life be completely about the children. They should join your life as opposed to you becoming their lives. Do your best to keep your life the way it was before kids as much as possible." — Bruce — Redondo Beach, Calif.

"A new dad can feel like a spectator not knowing how to get involved. Ask your partner to point you in the right direction if you're lost. Let her know how much you want to help. The more involved Dad is, the sooner

he can bond with his child and the happier the partnership." — Jim — Dallas, Texas

"Don't let the kids take over. Make your relationship the most important thing to each other. Get out as soon as possible. Have a special date at least once a month to keep the romance going." — Sam — San Francisco, Calif.

"Keep your eyes open and be curious. Ask questions even in areas where you feel you'll get your head bitten off. If you have an idea about your partner's feelings ask if you're picking up the correct signal. Asking the questions opens the door for better communication." — Stewart — Brentwood, Calif.

"Maintain a good sense of humor throughout your parenting experience—especially in the first year." — Bob — Westlake, Calif.

Miss me? As simple as this last statement is, it speaks a great truth. Although lack of sleep, middle-of-the-night feedings, baby vomit on all your clothes, arguing siblings, very little sex, and different parenting philosophies may not seem so funny, you must find a place for humor. Raising children *can* be overwhelming. If you can find the punch line amidst the stress, share it out loud and have a good laugh together. If you can't see the humor, look harder. Believe me, it's there.

"Having a child is an incredible burden at first and you've got to remember it won't always be that way. Help ease the burden by giving each other breaks." — John — Malibu, Calif.

"Respect each other. You're both doing the best you can with what you know. When you respect your partner and don't ridicule her for mistakes, she'll keep giving you her best." — Joe — Agoura, Calif.

"Look at the way you used to do things and be willing to change whatever needs changing to make your lives easier. Look inside yourself and see where you can improve. Ask your partner what you can do to be a better parent and partner. Be willing to hear him or her or don't bother asking." — Jeff — Van Nuys, Calif.

"Most parents realize they need to have patience with their kids. Having patience with your partner is very important now, too. You're both learning so much, so quickly. Accept each others mistakes with love and support." — Mike — Whittier, Calif.

"The reason your kids exist is because of the two of you. Enjoy your time with them but remember, they will grow up and need you less. Ideally, your partner will be with you when the kids are gone. Never lose sight of that." — Jason —Dallas, Texas

"It's easy for a dad to feel jealous in the first few weeks believing he's lost his partner to the child. Speak up. Share your feelings without being upset." — Ken — Ventura, Calif.

"Try to maintain doing the things you enjoyed in your life before kids. With all the changes kids bring, it's important to hold onto something that keeps you feeling special about your relationship with your partner." — Mark — San Diego, Calif.

"Have as much patience as you can with the change in your sex life. It will be gone for a while and it's never quite the same as it was before children. Talk about this openly and know that there will be a day when you're back on track again." — Joel — Moorepark, Calif.

"After children, you'll learn things about your partner you never knew. Some of these new traits you might not like. Because of this, it's vital to remember the person you married and all the things you love about her." — Adam — Englewood, N.J.

By now you've probably realized that it's just not possible for me to disappear for too many pages. Until we have children, a big part of our childhood lies in the shadows. If you're discovering new things about your wonderful mate since the birth of your child, chances are, you're witnessing behavior instilled from her parents. If you like this discovery, give a compliment. If you don't, find the appropriate time to ask a few questions about the way she was raised. Perhaps her parents responded to her the way she reacts to your child or to you. If she's unaware of her pattern, bring it to her awareness to help her avoid the same reaction next time. Once again, this is about you understanding instead of needing to be understood. (The word "she" can certainly be replaced with the word "he" in the above paragraph.)

Having our own children will continuously reveal many things about our pasts. Just keep discovering and then create your own blueprint.

"You don't have to fix your partner's feelings. You don't even have to understand them all the time. Just be willing to listen to help ease the pressure of mothering." — Philip — Altadena, Calif.

"Remember to say I love you as much as possible. Hug your partner, thank her, and get involved right from the start." — Tony — Dallas, Texas

"Say thank you, thank you, thank you. Never stop appreciating your partner." — Mark — Sherman Oaks, Calif.

"Marriage after children is a physical and mental task of labor. Like building a house, you need a strong foundation to keep things from collapsing when there's too much stress. Work extra hard at strengthening your foundation when you have kids. Continue checking for little cracks along the way to avoid the big ones that destroy the foundation." — Paul — Newport Beach, Calif.

I couldn't have said it better myself. Thank you, Paul.

Well, there you have it. Some great wisdom from some very wise parents. Remember to refresh your memory with these tidbits by reading them over and over again. They really do make a lot of sense.

My apologies once again for not being able to keep my mouth shut (make that, keep my fingers off the keyboard) for more than one page at a time.

Closing

Your life no longer involves just you and your partner. You chose to take on the responsibility of creating a new life. This decision isn't to be taken lightly. There is no doubt that having children can turn a relationship into complete chaos and leave both of you feeling helpless at times. There is also no doubt in my mind that if you want your family to grow intellectually, emotionally, and spiritually, you can make that happen, too.

How long it takes to get there is not important. As long as the steps you're taking are moving you forward, you will be well on your way to the happiness you deserve.

You must be willing to look deep into your heart because this is where all the real answers lie. It was in your heart that you decided to fall in love, and it was in your heart that you made the decision to have a child together.

Perhaps, as you were reading this book, you found some of the answers you've been looking for. The truth is, they were already a part of you and the words just brought them up from your heart to your consciousness.

Although you're individuals, deep down you have a common goal: to give your child the best life possible. Why not give each other the best life possible? Your partner deserves your very best, too. How you do this is quite simple: with love and with an honest commitment to your relationship. Remember what first brought the two of you together and move forward from that place.

You are two human beings with many differences. These differences don't mean one person is right and the other is wrong. All they mean is that there's more than one way to look at life. Explore your differences as you raise your child and learn from each other. Notice what each of you have to offer to your family and take the very best of both.

I'd like to leave you with one last thought. Take a look at your child or children as they lay sleeping and think about this: as a couple, you created a miracle. Not just because you brought a child into the world but because you created *that* child. There is no other combination of people in the universe who could have possibly given life to your son or daughter. Now, knowing how much you love that little miracle, would you be willing to gratefully tell your partner how glad you are that he or she is in your life? And while you're doing that, how about throwing in an, "I love you." Your children learn the lesson of walking by watching you; let them learn the lesson of love by watching you, too.

May the two of you create love and harmony and

embrace each other from the deepest part of your souls. May you lead the way for your family to grow and prosper into everything you ever dreamed possible.

To Betsy

Ric Giardina

You tend our child with love. With grace

So pure, the angels stand amazed, attendant

As they are on God. No day triumphant

Yet everyday a triumph in itself.

Though worlds apart, adult and child,

Each day some new mature awareness,

Placed there by you, glows in her unfledged eyes,

Just as in you each day with her your Child awakes.

What special gifts you bring to her! To me,

In seeing you and her and you in her. A thousand-fold

My love for you has grown since we were just we two

And thought to share our love with someone yet unknown.

My heart is full. With love for you. For her. For us.

That we, together, did create this miracle she is.

©1996, Ric Giardina, All Rights Reserved

Afterword

I understand how enormous the transition is when children enter your life. To say it's not always easy is the understatement of the species. It's taken my husband and me an immense amount of work to get to where we are in our relationship and quite honestly, there were moments when I questioned if we were going to make it. We did and we will never stop working on us.

The suggestions in this book have worked for my relationship and many other parents I've shared them with. However, I don't have all the answers. No one does.

Your situation may require deeper work than I was able to bring forth. If your partner is unwilling to hear you, talk to you, or participate in raising your family, it would be wise for you to seek professional counseling.

If he or she is resistant about going, then go by yourself. It can still be effective. How do I know this? I went alone. I took it upon myself to make the changes in *me*, instead of Jim, and by doing so, he changed too. I shared with Jim, from my sessions, what I believed would fuel our relationship—and it worked. Other times I just changed my attitude from bad to good and that's all it took to make a shift in the way we interacted as a family.

If you grew up with some major dysfunctions in your family then it's vital you seek the assistance you need so you don't repeat the same problems with your partner and children.

This is your opportunity to rip up the old blueprint and draw a whole new set of plans. You and your partner are the architects and together you can build a foundation that's strong enough to support anything that enters your life.

I'd love to hear from you. Please let me know how the book affected you individually and how it affected your relationship. Tell me what you used that worked for the two of you.

I'm available for speaking engagements and telephone consultations; or if you're interested in attending my workshop please call me. I love building new friendships, so don't be a stranger. I want to know who my readers are.

Linda Salazar
Parents In Love
P.O. Box 3501
Rolling Hills Estates, CA 90274
310-375-4800
or
888-90-FAMILY
E-mail: linda@parentsinlove.com
Website: http://www.parentsinlove.com

Coupon for
Parents In Love

This coupon entitles you to a day

to yourself from 9 A.M.—4 P.M.

To_____

With Love_____

- -

Coupon for
Parents In Love

This coupon entitles you to a day

to yourself from 9 A.M.—4 P.M.

To_____

With Love_____

Coupon for
Parents In Love

This coupon is good for one love making
session the way *you* want to make love!

To_____

With Love_____

- -

Coupon for
Parents In Love

This coupon is good for one love making
session the way *you* want to make love!

To_____

With Love_____

Coupon for
Parents In Love

This coupon entitles you and me to spend a day or evening together doing anything *you* want to do.

To_____

With Love_____

- -

Coupon for
Parents In Love

This coupon entitles you and me to spend a day or evening together doing anything *you* want to do.

To_____

With Love_____

Coupon for
Parents In Love

This coupon entitles you to all the hugs and kisses you want for an entire day.

To_____

With Love_____

- -

Coupon for
Parents In Love

This coupon entitles you to all the hugs and kisses you want for an entire day.

To_____

With Love_____

Coupon for
Parents In Love

This coupon entitles you to an entire morning to yourself.

To_____

With Love_____

- -

Coupon for
Parents In Love

This coupon entitles you to an entire morning to yourself.

To_____

With Love_____

Coupon for
Parents In Love

This coupon entitles you to an entire afternoon to yourself.

To_____

With Love_____

Coupon for
Parents In Love

This coupon entitles you to an entire afternoon to yourself.

To_____

With Love_____

Recommended Readings

Giving the Love that Heals: A Guide for Parents
&
Getting the Love You Want: A Guide for Couples
Helen Hendrix & Harville Hendrix Ph.D

The Couples Comfort Book
Jennifer Louden

How We Can Light A Fire When The Kids Are Driving Us Crazy
Ellen Kriedman

For Better Or Worse
Susan Squire

When Partners Become Parents
Cowan & Cowan

Love Secrets for a Lasting Relationship
&
Lifemates: The Love Fitness Program for a Lasting Relationship
Harold H. Bloomfield, Ph.D.

30 Secrets of Happily Married Couples
Dr. Paul Coleman

The Transition To Parenthood
Jay Belsky, Ph.D. & John Kelly

The Love You Deserve
Scott Peck

How To Stay Lovers While Raising Your Children
Anne Mayer

Keeping Love Alive
Tina Dayton

True Love
Daphne Rose Kingman

About the Author

Linda Salazar leads workshops helping couples deal with the changes in their relationships after having children. Her work has been featured in various media, such as The Los Angeles Times, LA Parent, and KCAL, Channel 9 news. Linda and her husband, Jim, have been married sixteen years and live in Los Angeles with Cosby, a dog, Raleigh, a cat, and of course, their son, Kyle—the influence and inspiration for *Parents In Love*. This is Linda's first book.

BOOK ORDERS

Phone Orders: Call (888) 90-Family
Fax Orders: Call (310) 375-4800

Mail Orders:
Kystar Publishing
P.O. Box 3501
Rolling Hills Estates, CA 90274

Please send me ____ copies of *Parents In Love*

Name: _____

Address: _____

City: _____

State: _____   Zip: _____

Telephone: _____

Price: $11.95 + $3.00 Postage and Handling

Sales Tax: Please add 8.25% for books shipped to California addresses

Payment:
___ Check   ___ Money Order   ___ Visa   ___ MC

Card number: _____

Print name on card: _____

Exp. date: ____/____

Signature: _____

Call toll *free* and order now

10% of all profits will be donated to children's charities